The
Money
Zone

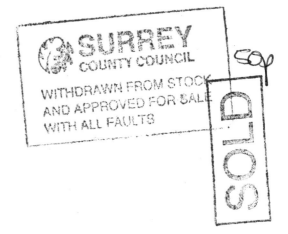

FINANCIAL TIMES

Prentice Hall

In an increasingly competitive world, it is quality
of thinking that gives an edge. An idea that opens new
doors, a technique that solves a problem, or an insight
that simply helps make sense of it all.

We work with leading authors in the fields of
management and finance to bring cutting-edge thinking
and best learning practice to a global market.

Under a range of leading imprints, including
Financial Times Prentice Hall, we create world-class
print publications and electronic products giving readers
knowledge and understanding which can then be
applied, whether studying or at work.

To find out more about our business and professional
products, you can visit us at www.business-minds.com

For other Pearson Education publications, visit
www.pearsoned-ema.com

Pearson
Education

Debbie Harrison

The
Money
Zone

FINANCIAL TIMES
Prentice Hall

an imprint of Pearson Education

London • New York • San Francisco • Toronto • Sydney
Tokyo • Singapore • Hong Kong • Cape Town • Madrid
Paris • Milan • Munich • Amsterdam

PEARSON EDUCATION LIMITED

Head Office:
Edinburgh Gate
Harlow CM20 2JE
Tel: +44 (0)1279 623623
Fax: +44 (0)1279 431059

London Office:
128 Long Acre
London WC2E 9AN
Tel: +44 (0)20 7447 2000
Fax: +44 (0)20 7240 5771
Website: www.business-minds.com

_____

First published in Great Britain in 2000

This publication is designed to provide accurate and authoritative information in
regard to the subject matter covered. It is sold with the understanding that neither
the author nor the publisher is engaged in rendering legal, investing, or any other
professional service. If legal advice or other expert assistance is required, the service
of a competent professional person should be sought.

ISBN 0 273 64504 8

British Library Cataloguing in Publication Data
A CIP catalogue record for this book can be obtained from the British Library.

10 9 8 7 6 5 4 3 2 1

Designed by Claire Brodmann Book Designs, Burton-on-Trent
Typeset by Northern Phototypesetting Co. Ltd, Bolton
Printed and bound in Great Britain by Biddles Ltd, Guildford & King's Lynn

The Publishers' policy is to use paper manufactured from sustainable forests.

About the author

Debbie Harrison is an award-winning financial author and journalist. She is a regular contributor to the *Financial Times*, *Bloomberg Money* and *Investment Week*. Her consumer titles include *Pension Power*, *First Time Investor* and *Personal Financial Planner* – all published by Financial Times Prentice Hall. She is also the author of five Financial Times management reports on UK and international pensions.

Acknowledgements

The film quotations used throughout this book were provided by The Internet Movie Database – a treasure trove for movie lovers. The website is at http://uk.imbd.com

All film stills are courtesy of Canal+Image UK Ltd.

Contents

Value this time in your life kids, because this is the time in your life when you still have your choices, and it goes by so quickly. When you're a teenager you think you can do anything, and you do. Your twenties are a blur. Your thirties you raise your family, you make a little money and you think to yourself, 'What happened to my twenties?' Your forties, you grow a little pot belly and you grow another chin. The music starts to get too loud and one of your old girlfriends from highschool becomes a grandmother. Your fifties, you have minor surgery. You'll call it a procedure but it's surgery. Your sixties, you'll have major surgery, the music is still loud but it doesn't matter because you can't hear it anyway. Seventies, you and the wife retire to Lauderdale, you start eating dinner at two, lunch around ten and breakfast the night before. And you spend most of your time wandering around malls looking for the ultimate in soft yoghurt and muttering, 'how come the kids don't call?' By your eighties you've had a major stroke and you end up babbling to some Jamaican nurse who your wife can't stand but who you call mama. Any questions?

Mitch Robbins, *City Slickers* (1991)

Preface

La dolce vita

Despite their own wild and woolly student days, parents have a habit of linking happiness to three financial objectives which they still reckon are pretty cool:

- get a steady job, preferably for life
- buy a house
- look after the pennies and the pounds will look after themselves.

They are, of course, wrong on all three counts.

Unlike flares, steady jobs for life went out in the 1970s and will not be coming back. Ever. What about that house? Well, buying might be a good idea but only if you know you are going to stay put for at least five years. Otherwise you're on to a loser. As for those pennies? Simple. If you spend your time looking after pennies, that's what you will end up with.

Money is fun to spend but after that it gets boring. The same is true of all that other financial planning stuff grown-ups fret and sweat about. What, you might well ask, is the point of life assurance if you don't get a life?

You're right, of course. But look at it this way. Most students leave university with debts of £10,000 – often a lot more. In those hippy-dippy days of the 1960s your parents didn't have that problem so they don't understand.

If you are not careful you could spend your twenties paying the government for the privilege of your higher education. Alternatively, if you get a bit organized, you could get a great job, rent a cool flat with some friends, and even start your own business and make some real money while having fun.

The point is that with minimal planning you can get the life you want now – not in 15 years' time when you will be too tired to enjoy it.

Read this book and kiss the long goodbye to your financial hassles. You will not be bored by economics or bamboozled by statistics. Instead you will learn to shoot from the hip, financially speaking, and avoid the big mistakes your parents probably made but are too embarrassed to mention.

This book will also help you keep it legal. If all else fails, however, remember Paul Newman's immortal words in *Butch Cassidy and the Sundance Kid* (1969), 'You know it could be worse. You get a lot more for your money in Bolivia, I checked on it.'

Debbie Harrison
May 2000

MUST   BE
CASH
&
DRIVE AWAY

Debt before dishonour

The **main** thing is to have **money**. I've been **rich** and I've been **poor**. **Believe** me *rich is better.*

Debby Marsh, *The Big Heat* (1953)

[Still from *School for Scoundrels*, Canal+Image UK Ltd]

chapter 1

Student days:
Swimming
with the
loan sharks

How much money
did you give
that guy?
A wiseguy never
pays for his drinks.

Lefty, *Donnie Brasco* (1997)

After reading this chapter you will:

- have a degree in student loans if nothing else;

- ditch the idea of going to college;

- rob a bank instead.

There's no such thing as a free lunch – or free education for that matter. Higher education is open to everyone, provided you can pay. These days borrowing is the name of the game and good old-fashioned grants things of the past. Shame.

If you want to go to university or college it is likely to cost you and/or your parents about £7,000 a year – more if you live in London.

You can borrow most of this through the Student Loan Company (SLC). The interest rates on the loan are called 'preferential' because the government in its generosity has decided that financial institutions should not make too much of a profit out of the students it has forced to pay for their full-time higher education.

However, the chickens come home to roost in the April after you have finished college (earlier if you drop out). This is when you have to start to repay your debts, provided you earn over about £10,000 a year.

Wealth warning!

People out there may try to sell you financial products that invest in volatile stockmarkets. Forget it. During the college years and the first few years afterwards your priority will be shedding your debt – not getting a mortgage, a tax-efficient savings plan or starting a pension.

In this chapter you will find out how the loan and assisted-fees system works. You will also

Oh, I see, then it was **murder.**
Will you marry me?
Did he **leave you**
any **money?**
Answer the **second** question **first.**

Rufus T Firefly, *Duck Soup* (1933)

discover how the government calculates the amount you can afford to pay once you finish your course. At the end of the chapter is a list of contacts for further research and a few tried and tested books that may help you through your student days.

Student debt

First the good news. The government (well, your tax-paying parents, actually) still pays about three-quarters of the bill for your university education. Typically, a full-time course costs about £4,000 a year and the government puts about £3,000 towards it.

The bad news is that this leaves two gaping holes:

- your contribution to tuition fees
- your living costs.

Your new best friend at this point is your local education authority (LEA), which handles the applications for tuition fee support, student loans and supplementary grants. You can find the number in the phone book under your local council. If you want to handle your LEA successfully, abandon all shyness and delicacy right now. Where a grant is means tested the LEA will ask you for lots of personal details about

your own and your parents' income, if applicable. Tell them to mind their own business and you will be a very poor student. For details on how to apply to your LEA, *see* page 10.

Tuition fees

Ever since the 1998–9 academic year, most full-time students starting courses of higher education have had to make a contribution towards their tuition fees. As a very rough

Mean money
When it comes to student loans, 'London' refers to the area covered by the City of London and the Metropolitan Police District. If you live half a mile outside this patch, tough – you will get the 'elsewhere' rate.

Let me tell you **one** thing son.
Noooobody ever lends money
to a man with a sense of humour.

Peter Tork, *Head* (1968)

guide, if your family's gross income is more than £23,000 you will have to make a modest contribution and if the total exceeds about £35,000 you are likely to have to pay the maximum contribution of over £1,000. In 1999–2000 the maximum contribution towards fees was £1,025 and this figure usually rises in line with inflation.

Some courses charge lower fees. These include:

- sandwich courses where a placement lasts a whole year or spans two academic years
- part-time teacher-training courses
- UK courses where you are required to spend a whole year studying in an overseas college.

In certain cases tuition may be free whatever your family's income – for example teacher training for work in the public sector. The government also helps out if you go into the armed forces – which is a much safer job these days than teaching.

Apply promptly for help with fees

As soon as you have an offer of a place at college or university – even if it is only conditional – apply to your LEA for help with fees and for your living costs loan (*see* page 10). Remember, if you apply late the loan may not be through in time for the start of term. If you don't expect to qualify for a loan, still make your application, otherwise you may lose your right to any help with tuition fees.

Tuition fees have to be paid for each year or term upfront – you can't build up credit and expect to pay after you have finished your course. Most colleges accept the fees in

Mean money
The chickens come home to roost in the April after you have finished college. This is when you have to start to repay your student loan.

box 1.1

How to make an extra buck – legally

Students using the NatWest website have been posting ideas to make and save cash:

1 Volunteer for drug trials/medical experimentation.

2 Take part in police identification line-ups.

3 Ask for presents in cash.

4 Shower together.

5 Go busking.

6 Pretend Monopoly money is real cash.

7 Enter all free prize draws.

8 Participate in market research/focus groups.

9 Marry a rich person.

10 Travel forward in time to know which shares to buy.

Source: NatWest web site: www.natwest.co.uk *The NatWest Student Guide: Your guide to managing money* is available from all NatWest branches.

instalments. However, following changes introduced in 1999, Scottish students no longer have to pay tuition fees upfront and instead make repayments once they have graduated.

Scottish students do not have to pay for their fees in their fourth year at university if the degree course is the equivalent of a three-year course in other parts of the UK. However, English students studying at a Scottish university do have to pay fourth-year fees. Check with your LEA and contact the Scottish office Education Department (*see* page 17).

European Union students

If you are a non-UK national of a European Union (EU) country you may get support for your tuition fees on a similar basis to UK students. However, in this case you will be sent an application form when you are offered a place by a college. All applications are dealt with by the Department for Education and Employment (DfEE – *see* page 17). In these circumstances the DfEE undertakes the same functions for EU students as the LEA does for UK students. However, as an EU student you will not be able to apply for a student loan, supplementary grants, a hardship loan or access funds.

Living costs

Apart from you and your family's own private resources, depending on your circumstances you can apply for three types of financial support to cover your living costs:

- loans
- supplementary grants for students in particular circumstances
- hardship loans and 'access funds'.

These loans are offered on an annual basis so you have to reapply each year. Again, your first port of call is the LEA.

Loans

This is the main source of help. Student loans are available to help meet your living costs while you are studying. Interest is pegged to the rate of inflation so this is a much cheaper source than the commercial banks or other lenders, which will charge a higher rate of interest in order to make profits for their shareholders.

Mean money

If you want to handle your LEA successfully, abandon all shyness and delicacy right now. The LEA will ask you for lots of personal information about your own and your parents' income. Tell them to mind their own business and you will be a very poor student.

You should apply to your LEA for your living costs loan at the same time that you apply for help towards your tuition fees. The LEA will tell you the maximum loan to which you are entitled and ask you how much of this maximum you require. You should then tell the Student Loan Company (SLC) what you have agreed. The SLC is responsible for actually transferring the money into your account at the beginning of each term (*see* below and page 17).

Most students will automatically qualify for about three-quarters of the maximum loan. The remaining quarter is means tested, so whether you qualify will depend on your own income and, where relevant, the income of your parents. Maximum loans are higher for students who have to study for extra weeks or who are required by their course to study overseas.

So why not go for the maximum allowed? Well, it is important to bear in mind that this is a *loan* not a grant, so whatever you borrow you will have to repay. If you borrow the maximum amount for London, for example, you could end up owing over £12,000 by the time you finish your course. Clearly then, you should only borrow what you really need and count yourself very lucky if you have generous parents. However, the thrifty should note that if you accept less than the maximum you cannot ask for the rest later. (They really don't make this easy.)

How the loan is calculated

The size of the loan depends on several factors, including where you live while you are at college, the type and length of course and your family's contribution. Table 1.1 shows the maximum basic loans for 2000–2001. Seventy-five per cent of this does not depend on your family's income and is shown in brackets. The loan is lower in the final year of study because it does not cover the summer holiday.

Additional grants and loans

There are additional sources of means-tested support for those in particularly difficult circumstances. Once again, apply through the LEA (or the DfEE if you are an EU student).

Supplementary grants

If you are disabled or have dependants you might qualify for extra help. Ask for details from the LEA if you already claim:

- dependants' allowance

- disabled students' allowances (DSAs – *see* page 13)

Table 1.1 Maximum basic student loans for 2000–2001 (non-means tested element in brackets)

	Full year	Final year
Students living away from home and studying in London	4,590 (3,445)	3,980 (2,985)
Students living away from home and studying elsewhere	3,725 (2,795)	3,230 (2,425)
Students living at home	2,950 (2,215)	2,575 (1,935)

Notes: 'London' refers to the area covered by the City of London and the Metropolitan Police District. If you live half a mile outside this patch, tough – you will get the 'elsewhere' rate. If you study abroad for eight or more weeks in a row during any academic year as a compulsory part of your course, you may be eligible for a higher loan. If your course lasts longer than the standard 38 weeks you may be able to get an additional means-tested loan to cover each academic week. The weekly supplement is: London £86, 'elsewhere' £65, parental home £45.

- travel allowance
- care leavers' grant.

Mean money
Borrow only what you really need and count yourself very lucky if you have generous parents.

Hardship loans and access funds

Hardship loans and access funds are available to students who have serious financial worries and might otherwise not be able to start or continue in higher education. They are not worth a hill of beans and you have to prove dire poverty to qualify.

Contributions from you and your family

Where the LEA decides you or your family should pay towards the costs of higher education the amount will first be put towards your fee contribution and then set against any dependants' allowance for which you are eligible. After this it will be put towards the means-tested part of your loan and finally against any travel grant for which you are eligible. Your family's contribution will not be set against any non-means-tested support for which you are eligible, such as disabled students' allowance, and most of the student loan.

Your new best friend – the LEA

If you have not already received one, ask your LEA for a copy of the booklet *Financial Support for Students*. You should also receive an application form so you can apply for fee support and your loan as soon as you have an offer of a place at university or college. Remember, it is important to apply even if the offer is conditional. If you delay you may start term with no money and if you leave it any later than four months after the beginning of term you will miss the boat completely.

Your LEA is a paper fiend. Its mission in life is to fell rainforests. To help it achieve this goal it will send you the following forms:

- an application form to assess your eligibility for student support;
- a notification form to confirm your eligibility;
- a financial form to assess the amount of support you are entitled to and what contribution you and your family will be expected to make;
- a notification form that tells you exactly how much support you will get;
- a loan request form to allow you to tell the SLC how much of your loan entitlement you want to take out.

Before it releases the loan, the SLC will want to see, among other items, your birth certificate, passport, and your national insurance number, as well as notification from the LEA. It will also need details of your bank account. If you haven't got a bank account yet, *see* Chapter 2.

How income is taken into account

Your income

When you complete the financial form the LEA will ask for an estimate of your income for the following year, including earned income and unearned income (from savings, investments, property and so on) and social security benefits. It will ignore the following income, which will not affect your entitlement:

- the first £1,000 from any scholarship, sponsor or award;
- the first £1,000 from your permanent employer if they are releasing you on full or part pay to attend college;
- any income from casual or part-time jobs during your course – for example evening jobs during term time or holiday jobs;
- National Health Service bursaries;
- the first £1,855 in trust income, depending on your circumstances;
- any payment made under the teacher-training initiative;
- most social security payments that are not taxed;
- any educational payments such as student

loans and payments from access funds (*see* page 10);
- the first £820 from any other source.

Your family's income

Your parents' income will be taken into account as well, unless you are treated as an independent student – for example, if you have been married for more than two years, you are over 25, or you have supported yourself for over three years. If your folks refuse to fill out the form, depending on the reasons, your LEA may not help you with your fees and loan application. If your parents no longer live together the LEA will assess whichever they think more suitable (probably the one with the deepest pockets). Married students will also be assessed on their spouse's income even if they have worked and paid their own taxes for several years. Unfair perhaps, but these are the rules.

Repayment of the loan

You are not expected to start paying back your loan until the April after you have finished your course (or left for other reasons, if this is earlier), and only then if you earn more than £10,000 (the threshold for 1999–2000). Interest will still be added to the loan at the rate of inflation.

If you earn above the threshold you must start to pay 9 per cent of the chunk of your annual salary above this amount to the SLC until the debt is cleared. Payments are deducted by your employer or, if you are self-employed, they are collected through the tax system. Don't think you can escape if you work overseas because the Inland Revenue has a very long arm indeed.

There is no fixed-time period for repayment. If you are on low earnings then the amount you repay each year will be correspondingly low and the repayment period that much longer.

If your annual income is less than £10,000 a year (in 1999–2000) the SLC will review your circumstances from time to time to try to catch you when you fall into their net. Bear in mind that if you receive over £2,000 in unearned income – from savings for example – this is also taken into account in the calculation of your repayment instalments.

Mean money
Don't think you can escape repayment of the loan if you work overseas. The Inland Revenue has a very long arm indeed.

Table 1.2 Student loan repayment calculation for graduate earning £12,000 p.a.

Monthly income	£1,000
Income on earnings below the threshold	£833
Income liable to assessment	£167
Monthly repayment (9% of £167)	£15

Note: The example assumes your income is spread evenly over the year.

Source: Department for Education and Employment

Table 1.3 Student loan repayment calculation for graduate earning £18,000 p.a.

Monthly income	£1,500
Income on earnings below the threshold	£833
Income liable to assessment	£667
Monthly repayment (9% of £667)	£60

Note: The example assumes your income is spread evenly over the year.

Source: Department for Education and Employment

Table 1.4 Loan repayments as a percentage of total monthly income

Annual income (£)	Payment per month (£)	% total income
up to 10,000	nil	nil
11,000	7	0.8
12,000	15	1.5
15,000	37	3
17,000	52	3.7
20,000	75	4.5

Can't pay, won't pay?

There's no legal way to avoid repaying your student loan apart from the rather drastic solution of dying young. However, if you are unfortunate enough to face a partial or total lifetime of earning less than the threshold or if you become disabled and cannot work, the slate is finally wiped clean when you reach the ripe old age of 65. Until then the dear old Revenue will keep tabs on you in case your earnings from begging or busking make you a worthwhile target.

Additional sources of finance

Disabled students

It is important to let your LEA know straightaway if you have a disability or learning difficulty (dyslexia, for example) and think you will need extra help or equipment to be able to attend your course. If you are eligible for fee support you may be able to get extra funding through the disabled students' allowances (DSAs). These allowances are not means tested and cover the following aspects:

- the specialist equipment allowance – this is worth up to £4,055 for the entire course and can be used for items like special furniture or a computer;

- the non-medical helpers' allowance – this is worth up to £10,250 a year and is used towards paying any helpers you need to benefit fully from your course, for example sign-language interpreters or notetakers;

- the general disabled students' allowance – this is worth up to £1,350 a year and is expected to cover any costs related to your disability for study purposes, for example tapes, books or Braille paper. You can also use it to top up the other two allowances.

On top of this your LEA may help towards extra travel costs due to your disability, provided these costs relate to your course.

Sponsorship

Some companies sponsor students through college and pay them to work during the holidays. You may find the prospect restrictive, particularly if you have to agree to work for the company for a minimum period after graduating. On the other hand, you may decide that financial support is a real blessing and removes a serious financial worry from your shoulders.

Historically, sponsorship tended to be restricted to engineering and science students. Today, opportunities also arise for students studying for degrees linked to commerce, such as economics, banking and accounting, or to computing. For further details *see* page 17.

If you are interested in joining the armed forces you may qualify for a sponsorship or bursary. Contact your local Armed Forced Careers Office.

Finally, a potential source of additional cash for performing arts students is the Arts Council.

box 1.2

Ten (more serious) ways to make the most of your money at college

1 Speak to your student adviser early to plan your finances.
2 Live in university accommodation whenever possible.
3 Claim all valuable discounts using your NUS card.
4 Shop for food with friends – buying in bulk can save money.
5 Eat on campus in the student union rather than in bars and restaurants.
6 Have a weekly budget – and try to stick to it.
7 Get a part-time job – as long as it doesn't interfere with your studies.
8 Keep a regular check on your bank account balance.
9 Buy your course books second hand.
10 Cycle to your lectures rather than paying for the bus.

Source: NatWest web site: www.natwest.co.uk

Bribery for urgently needed skills

Teachers

There's a general shortage of teachers. Not surprising really when you consider that this is now classed as a high risk occupation like professional bungee jumping and gun running in Sicily.

The shortage is most acute where it involves doing clever stuff like adding up and taking away. To encourage students to train as teachers, those on Postgraduate Certificate in Education (PGCE) courses do not have to pay fees. You also get extra brownie points if you are prepared to teach maths at a state school. The level of the bribe here is £5,000, half of which is paid when you start an appropriate course and the other half when you take up a post at a maintained secondary school. There is a sticky end to the lollipop of course – the bribe is treated as taxable income.

Medics

There's also a shortage of medics. Again, this is not surprising when you consider the things they have to do before and even during breakfast. The National Health Service offers bursaries for health professional courses. Your LEA should automatically provide information if you apply for fee support and a loan for this type of course.

Career development loans

If you cannot get any student support through your LEA you may be able to apply for a career development loan (CDL). The DfEE manages these loans through partnerships with several high-street banks to support courses in a wide range of vocational subjects. Needless to say the banks want their pound of flesh, so the terms are not as good as you get for student loans, but are likely to be better than if you look independently. If you are over 18 you can apply for a CDL worth up to £8,000 to cover up to 80 per cent of your course fees plus other related costs.

Not satisfied?

Well, if you made it through this chapter you may be a little the wiser about student loans but you will also appreciate just how complicated the system is. This is not helped by the fact that you have to deal with several

Mean money
The government is more generous if you train to become a teacher. Though there are safer jobs – like professional bungee jumping and teaching Mafia inmates wickerwork.

authorities, including your college, the LEA, the DfEE, the SLC, and the Inland Revenue (give yourself a pat on the back if you remember what the acronyms stand for).

Needless to say, sometimes things go wrong. This may be due to a delay in one particular department or because someone, somewhere screws up. If you are unhappy with the service or decision made by one of the authorities, ask for details of their complaints system. They should offer you an independent review if you are still not satisfied after your complaint has been investigated. The reviewer is likely to be one of the following:

- LEA complaints – the Local Government Ombudsman
- central government including the DfEE – the Parliamentary Ombudsman
- the SLC – the SLC Assessor
- Inland Revenue complaints (regarding repayments of the loan) – the Revenue Adjudicator.

Summary

- If you want to go to university or college it will cost about £7,000 a year.
- You can borrow most of this, but the majority of students still end up with more debt than their student loan.
- Don't borrow more than you need – if you take the maximum you could be £12,000 in debt by the end of your course.
- Special professions get extra financial help – teachers, medics, the armed forces.
- Check if a company will sponsor you through college/university.
- You start to repay your student loan the April after you finish.
- Don't buy any savings and investment products until you are clear of debt.

Further information

Contacts

Access funds and hardship loans: ask your college for information, but only if you think you can convince them you are in dire straits.

The Arts Council's Education and Training Department may provide financial help for performing arts students (020 7333 0100).

Department for Education and Employment, Mowden Hall, Staindrop Road, Darlington, Co. Durham DL3 9BG. For *Financial Support for Students*, call freefone 0800 210 280 or visit their website www.dfee.gov.uk For the free booklet on career development loans call freefone 0800 585 505 between 9 am and 9 pm Monday to Friday. Alternatively, you may need to call the Student Awards Agency for Scotland on 0131 476 8212; the Department of Education for Northern Ireland on 028 9127 9279; or the Welsh Office Education Department on 029 2082 5831.

Disabled students' allowance: for details call freefone 0800 731 9133.

Educational Grants Advisory Service (EGAS): if you are unable to get funding for further education EGAS, an independent advice agency, may be able to help. Send an SAE to EGAS, 501–505 Kingsland Road, Dalston, London E8 4AU or telephone the information line on 020 7249 6636.

Local Education Authority (LEA): you will find the number in the telephone book under your local council.

NHS bursaries: contact your college or one of the following, depending on where you are studying: England – the NHS Student Grants Unit (01253 856 123); Wales – the Welsh Health Common Services Agency (029 2082 5111); Scotland – the Student Awards Agency for Scotland (0131 476 8212); Northern Ireland – Department of Education for Northern Ireland (028 9127 9279).

National Union of Students, 461 Holloway Road, London N7 6LJ (020 7272 8900; www.nus.org.uk).

Scottish Office Education Department: telephone for copies of *Investing in the Future: Supporting Students in Higher Education*: 0131 556 8400.

Social security: ask your Department of Social Security for leaflet FB 23 *Young people's guide to social security* and *see* page 71.

Student information: try www.studentpages.com – details of entertainment, shopping and money saving facilities around UK universities, plus how to join a freshers' service that offers free advice.

Student Loan Company Ltd: if you need to check the progress of your loan application contact the Student Loans Company at 100 Bothwell Street, Glasgow G2 7JD or telephone freefone 0800 405 010.

Books/leaflets

A quick way to order books, often at a discount, is through Amazon Bookshop: www.amazon.co.uk

Education Grants Directory, published by the Directory of Social Change, 24 Stephenson Way, London NW1 2DP.

A Guide to University Scholarships and Awards by Brian Heap, published by Trotman & Co. Ltd, 12 Hill Rise, Richmond TW10 6UA.

A question of sponsorship is free from the Student Sponsorship Information Services (SSIS), PO Box 36, Newton-Le-Willows, Merseyside WA12 0DW.

Sponsorship for Students, published by CRAC/Hobsons, available from Customer Services, Biblios PDS Ltd, Star Road, Partridge Green, West Sussex RH13 8LD.

Student Life – A Survival Guide, published by Hobsons Publishing plc, available from Customer Services, Biblios PDS Ltd, Star Road, Partridge Green, West Sussex RH13 8LD.

Students' Money Matters, published by Trotman &
   Co. Ltd, 12 Hill Rise, Richmond TW10 6UA
   (www.trotmanpublishing.co.uk).
Summer Jobs in Britain and *Summer Jobs Abroad*,
   published by Vacation Work, 9 Park End Street,
   Oxford OX1 1HJ, available from major
   bookshops.

chapter 2

Current
affairs

Whenever
we **needed**
money, we'd **rob**

the airport.

To us, it was

better than

Citibank.

Henry Hill, *Goodfellas* (1990)

After reading this chapter you will:

- know how to charm the socks off your bank by keeping in touch;

- recognize the difference between borrowing and stealing;

- decide to become a bank manager when you grow up.

Cash is an anachronism these days. It is much cooler to deal in credit and debit cards – which are the subject of the next chapter. Nevertheless we have a cash economy and we have to trust the stuff, otherwise the world would stop turning until the great powers decided which types of beads would do instead of coins and notes.

In the meantime the Student Loan Company will not hand over your money in a briefcase but will insist you open up an account to receive it. In fact you never get to see it. The bank will simply send you depressing statements to show how much you started with and how little you have left. If things get bad the bank might ask you to call in for a visit. Please note, this is not a friendly invitation.

You pays your money

Long gone is the monopoly of the three or four major high-street banks. Dozens of new providers have entered the market – including several major insurance companies and retail operations. This has done wonders for competition but it has also made the choice more difficult.

Rates of interest and banking services change frequently, so this chapter is not intended to provide an up-to-date review of offers. Once you have decided what type of account you are looking for, the best source of information on facilities, charges and rates of interest is *Moneyfacts* (*see* page 30).

Which type of account?

Banks adore students, believe it or not, and offer them perks to open an account. These are discussed on page 26. However, when the student and early postgraduate years are over, so are the perks. Even so, it is important to choose the standard account that best matches your requirements and expected cashflow.

Most banks offer three basic types of account, all of which will provide you with a range of plastic cards. Banking-related cards are explained on page 23. Credit cards are examined in the next chapter.

Interest-paying accounts

In the unlikely event you are organized and disciplined you probably don't need this book in the first place. But if you do fall into this category you might consider an account

Mean money

Your cashcard will have an identity number that you must keep secret. Don't write it in your diary or anywhere else in your purse or wallet. Pickpockets can spot an ID number at 1,000 paces – even if you have cunningly disguised it.

that expects you to remain in credit and pays a nominal rate of interest on the balance.

For years banks made excessive profits out of current accounts, partly because they did not have to pay interest on the balance. Your money was lent out – often overnight to other

When I put my mind to something, I go all the way. I'll go all the way for you sir. I'm a big fan of money. I have a little. I keep it in a jar on top of my refrigerator. I wanna put more in the jar. That's where you come in.

Robbie, *The Wedding Singer* (1998)

financial institutions – at a profit, and none of this was passed on to you.

Today many banks offer interest on current accounts, but frankly in most cases it isn't worth the candle. The big high-street banks tend to be the meanest here, but one or two of the more innovative banks do offer a reasonable rate. This may be an attractive feature if you happen to keep a high balance in your account, but for most students the overdraft terms are far more important. Besides, if you can manage the discipline, in most cases you would be better off shifting any surplus to a deposit account to earn a better rate of interest while you do not need the money.

Flexibility but no interest

The second and more traditional type of bank account does not pay interest but is a lot more accommodating if you need an overdraft – for example the charges will be lower than for the interest-paying account.

Fee accounts

For customers with above-average earnings most banks also offer an account that charges a fee – typically £6 a month. In return you get access to a range of facilities and discounted products.

The stated aim of these accounts is to provide a half-way house between high-street accounts and the sort of posh services offered by private banks for middle and higher earners. Of course the underlying aim is for banks to make more money out of their current-account customers.

Are they worth the money? The answer, as always, is that it depends. In some cases you will get useful banking-related facilities – for example lower borrowing rates, cheaper overdrafts and tiered interest rates on the balance in the account. Some accounts, however, will bombard you with a never-ending stream of non-banking products such as free or cheap travel insurance, cheap life assurance, air-miles points on purchases with their credit card and so on.

It's very tempting to become somebody's 'goldcard' customer, but before you do, make sure you are going to use the facilities or products regularly. The type of people who benefit from these accounts include frequent

Mean money
Frankly, the jury is still out on whether the levels of interest paid are worth the candle but over the past year or so newcomers have challenged the high-street old guard and offer quite competitive rates.

travellers who can make genuine savings on the free travel insurance and discounted flight or holiday prices, and those with a fairly high annual income but erratic cashflow, who find the low cost overdraft facility very attractive.

If, however, you pay all your credit bills on time, never have an overdraft and are unlikely to use the range of products on offer, then you would probably be better off with a standard bank account.

Internet banking

How sophisticated do you want your account to be? Banking via the Internet is the latest trend and already looks poised to replace telephone banking (while the latter is still in its infancy).

For many people the prospect of being able to carry out banking transactions 24 hours a day is very convenient and time saving. If you use the Internet rather than a dedicated PC/modem link, you can tap into your account from just about anywhere – the office, college, home and even a laptop on a train. However, you do need a decent computer, otherwise it can be a slow process.

Next in the evolutionary process will be mobile-phone banking using wireless application protocol (WAP) technology. Also coming up is banking via digital TV. However, for some – especially first-timers – there is still a comfort factor in knowing you can go into your local bank branch, most of which have online facilities. Once you have been working for a few years and have a reliable cashflow then it may well be worth exploring Internet banking. In the meantime, don't be pushed into buying any equipment for a dedicated modem line that may quickly become obsolete.

Banking facilities

The following section is a real back-to-basics for those who are opening their first account or who have already done so but never bothered to read the literature. If you have been there and done that, skip it.

Your bank cards

Broadly speaking cards fall into two basic categories – bank-account related, and credit cards. Credit cards are dealt with in the next chapter. Bank-account related cards include:

- *Cheque guarantee card*: guarantees to the vendor that the bank will honour your cheques up to the limit stated on the card – typically £100, £200 or £300 – even if there is nothing in your account. Most shops will not accept a cheque unless you can provide this type of card.

- *Cashpoint or automated teller card*: usually combines with the cheque guarantee card. You can use it to make withdrawals up to the limit on the card from any cashpoint ('hole in the wall') machine that serves your bank. You can also get an up-to-date balance and order a cheque book and a statement. For cash only you can use a huge range of machines as most banks have reciprocal arrangements with other card issuers. Your card will have an identity number that you must keep secret. Don't write it in your diary or anywhere else in your purse or wallet. Pickpockets can spot an ID number at 1,000 paces – even if you have cunningly disguised it.

- *Switch or debit card*: directly debits your account with the amount of your purchase. This type of card is rapidly replacing the cheque book.

Standing orders

A standing order is a handy way to pay for regular outgoings to the same individual or company. You fill out a form for the bank and it will pay the required amount into the company or person's own bank account, usually on the same day of each month.

Direct debit

Direct debit is used instead of a standing order if the amount is likely to vary from month to month – for example utility bills or a mortgage where the interest rate is not fixed and so will fluctuate.

With a direct debit the organization to which you wish to make the payment collects the money directly from your account, which is why you have to give written permission for the arrangement to both the bank and to the company that is collecting the money. To cancel a direct debit you need to inform both the bank and the company.

Bank charges

Banks will deduct charges from your account for certain transactions, depending on the type of account. If you are in credit all the time then you should not be charged for the issuing of statements, cheque books, withdrawals, stopping lost or stolen cheques, and general administration. If you are overdrawn usually the bank will charge for most transactions, either quarterly or per item.

In addition there are penalty charges, for example to cover interest payments on overdrafts or if you go overdrawn without prior authority. If you write a cheque for more than is in your account or for an amount that takes you over your overdraft limit the bank may refuse to pay up. This is known as a bounced cheque and you will pay dearly for the embarrassment.

Arranging an overdraft

If you need more money than you have in your account you will probably be able to borrow some from the bank up to a certain limit. There is usually a fixed fee for arranging an overdraft and interest is usually calculated on the overdraft on a daily basis and charged to your account at quarterly intervals. Banks usually expect overdrafts to be cleared within three to 12 months, or at the very least to be renegotiated.

The golden rule of good banking is to never go overdrawn without permission. Banks may be awash with cash but if you take what is not yours they will regard you as a thief and treat you like one.

Loans

Banks are keen to lend you money to the point where they will send you letters full of ideas for different ways to spend more than you earn – a new car, an extension to the house, a world cruise and so on. Of course you will have to pay interest on any loan – although not so much as you would if you borrow through a less reputable source (see page 33).

The golden rule of loans is don't take one out unless you can genuinely afford the repayments of capital and interest. If you do need a loan, check *Moneyfacts* for the best terms. You do not have to go to your own bank.

Pre-college years

More and more teenagers are opening bank accounts as parents decide to give them an

Mean money
Banking via the Internet is the latest trend and already looks poised to replace telephone banking.

allowance for clothes and spending, rather than a weekly hand-out in the form of pocket money. According to a straw poll survey among 11–12-year-olds, bank accounts, like mobile phones, are 'class', while pocket money is not.

In an attempt to catch young people before they fly the nest and go to college, some banks offer preferential rates to 16-year-olds and may even offer a debit card (see above). At the time of writing, Barclays 'Further Education' account, for example, offered up to £150 of retail discount vouchers for students in full-time education working towards A levels or their equivalent.

This type of marketing is very sound from the banks' point of view and represents a pre-emptive strike on students expected to go into higher education. The reasons for the perks are that if you are diligent in your studies you should prove to be a good earner in due course. Of course a closer look at the real world would reveal that 16-year-old leavers who go into employment tend to be much

American **millionaires**
must be all quite **mad**.
Perhaps it's **something**
they put in the **ink** when
they **print the money**.

Charles Bonnet, *How to Steal a Million* (1966)

potential than other young people – once they get out of the sex, drugs and rock and roll stage that is.

Moreover, despite the proliferation of new types of bank accounts, including telephone banking and banking on the Internet, most people join a bank when they go to college and never get round to changing it later. So banks reckon, with some justification, if they can catch you as a student, they've got you for life.

more diligent and responsible than university students. But there you go. Banks have deep pockets and can afford to take a very long-term view.

Apart from the perks, several banks offer decent rates of interest on young people's bank accounts, while some offer a cheque book and, from age 18, a cheque card.

Student bank accounts

After the Local Education Authority, if you are a student, your next best friend is likely to be your bank. The National Union of Students (NUS) reckons most students not only use up their loans but they also run up a bank overdraft of well over £1,000 each academic year. Some build up much bigger debts.

Fortunately, banks like students because they are good creditors and usually repay any debts at the agreed time. Students also are supposed to have much higher future-earning

The good news for students is that the banks compete fiercely for your custom. You may think you will make a poor customer, given the fact that you face many years of debt before you can really start making some dosh, but remember the banks love customers who are in debt because your impecuniosity is their profit. The more debt the merrier – always provided your bank agrees in the first place.

Comparing student accounts

Probably the best source of comparisons between different banks for students is the annual *Moneyfacts* student account survey. The 1999 offers available from NatWest, listed in box 2.1, give you an idea of what to expect. However, a totally new package will be

box 2.1

Student bank account offers

New students opening a NatWest Student Account before 30 November 1999 could choose between a cash gift of at least £35 or the latest Panasonic portable compact disc player. The 1999 student package included a further incentive for students to bank at one of NatWest's specialist Student and Graduate Banking Service branches by offering a bonus £15, bringing the cash gift to £50.

The package also included:

- interest-free overdraft for five years, up to £2,000 (no fees);
- NatWest MasterCard and Visa credit card on one account, with no annual fee for duration of study;
- student travel insurance with policies of up to 12 months; commission-free American Express traveller's cheques and foreign currency;
- NatWest On-Line – 30-day free trial and 50 per cent discount on the one-off set up charge of £30 for NatWest's PC banking package;
- belongings insurance – 10 per cent discount on first year's premium;
- access to one of 250 specialist student advisers around the country;
- professional trainee loan scheme – available to full-time second-year students studying for the governing bodies' qualifications, e.g. barrister, chiropodist, dentist, doctor.

launched in the summer of 2000 for students starting their courses in October 2000.

To qualify for student accounts you normally have to be coming up to your first term at college or university. You will have to prove your status – for example by showing the bank your Local Education Authority award offer or your first term's grant cheque.

Students must be getting more sensible and less likely to buy the cereal packets with the free gifts. In 1999 the banks dropped a lot of the fun goodies and instead offered new students a specialist advice service on campus, fee-free credit cards, commission-free traveller's cheques and currency, a mobile phone or a free railcard. Some offer a cash lump sum. In 1999 £50 was typical for the major high-street banks. One particularly generous offer came from Clydesdale which said it would pay all interest on a student loan accumulated while studying. This could be worth up to £500.

But whatever the temptation, do check that the costs of the basic services are competitive. Bear in mind you will be under pressure to sign up before a cut-off date to qualify for the perks, so don't let that push you into making the wrong decision.

Interest-free overdrafts

One of the most attractive features of a student account is that you should qualify for

Mean money
If you write a cheque for more than is in your account or for an amount that takes you over your overdraft limit, the bank may refuse to pay up. This is known as a bounced cheque and you will pay dearly for the embarrassment.

an interest-free overdraft. Since most banks offer this facility, do compare the terms, the overdraft limits, and the rate of interest charged if you exceed this maximum.

Banks used to dealing with students also tend to be quite sympathetic towards student debt generally, *provided* you keep in touch and warn them in advance if you are about to go into the red.

Bank student advisers

As mentioned above, the banks are keen to help students manage their money and several provide an adviser on campus who can answer your questions or help sort out problems for you. Remember though, these are not independent advisers – they will only give advice that relates to their own bank.

Location

Even if you plan to rely on a telephone, PC and/or Internet banking service, do make sure you have access to a branch at or very near either your college or your lodgings, particularly if this is your first bank account and your first attempt at living away from home. If you run into trouble or get confused it is easier to talk face-to-face rather than try to work out which computer voice service is most appropriate.

Low-cost graduate personal loans

A low-cost personal loan can be a real help for new graduates who seem to start their careers with nothing but debts. Equally, it can turn your bad debts into a nightmare if you are adding a chunky personal loan to your existing student loan.

Banks offer loans at preferential rates and may advance up to £5,000, although Midland and NatWest offer up to £10,000. Some banks link the loan to your earnings – for example 20 per cent of your starting salary.

Summary

- Banks love students and their debts, provided the students agree overdraft limits before going into the red.
- Look for the annual survey of student accounts in *Moneyfacts*.
- Avoid accounts that pay interest when you are in the black but impose heavy penalties if you accidentally overdraw – unless you are very disciplined.
- Avoid accounts that charge a fee, unless you genuinely can use the facilities on offer.
- If this is your first account, or if you are at college and likely to run into debt, make sure your bank has a convenient branch.

Further information

Moneyfacts: this is the main source of deposit account information as well as an excellent source for savings and mortgage products. Contact Moneyfacts, Moneyfacts House, 66–70 Thorpe Road, Norwich NR1 1BJ (01603 476476). e-mail: enquiries@moneyfacts.co.uk Moneyfacts is available only by annual subscription but you can buy a one-off copy for £5.95 by phone using your credit card. Tel 01603 476100. Some libraries do stock copies. Also useful sources are the personal finance pages of the weekend national newspapers.

Bank websites

It is worth visiting these websites when you are looking for a new student account:

Bank of Scotland: www.bankofscotland.co.uk
Barclays: www.barclays.co.uk
Lloyds TSB: www.lloydstsb.co.uk
Midland: www.midlandbank.com
NatWest: www.natwest.co.uk
Royal Bank of Scotland: www.rbos.co.uk

chapter 3

Plastic
fantastic
lovers

Nora, managing your money is so **easy**. You **use** your credit cards! You **pay** your American Express with your Discover, **your Discover** with your Visa, **your Visa** with your MasterCard. Before they catch up with you, you're **buried** in a glorious crypt in Bel-Air!

Camilla, *The Naked Truth* (1955)

After reading this chapter you will:

- understand why Dante confined the money lenders to the Seventh Circle of Hell;

- be able to identify your future life partner by his or her credit cards;

- still not understand how the annual percentage rate of interest is calculated.

This chapter deals with the respectable end of credit – the credit-card issuers, which command a market said to be worth £60 billion.

Respectable it may be, but the National Association of Citizens Advice Bureaux mops up the tears of some three-quarters of a million people with debt-related problems each year and half of these are to do with credit cards, store cards or other consumer credit arrangements.

So what is a credit card?

There's a lot of confusion about plastic cards – which is not surprising, given the number on the market (up from two to about 20 in the past few years) and the different functions they perform. One card will allow you to make virtually any purchase on credit, another will do the same thing but donate a few pence to a trade union for every purchase you make, while some give to charities. Yet others will allow you to buy goods on credit from certain stores.

Unlike banking cards, credit cards are not linked to your current account. Although they go by different names, broadly speaking there are two different types of card – a charge card and a credit card:

- *Charge cards* provide you with credit for up to a month but you are expected to repay the entire balance at the end of each month – most charge cards are available only to the issuing bank's current-account customers

(American Express and Diners Club International being the two chief exceptions);

- *Credit cards* require you to pay a minimum amount towards the balance each month – you do not have to pay off the entire amount but you will be charged interest on the remaining balance.

Bear in mind that nobody is obliged to give you credit and if you are turned down the company may have consulted a credit reference agency, which keeps records of people who do not pay their debts.

Why credit agencies love you

The credit company will assess your creditworthiness by considering your income and regular commitments. It will then set a maximum limit per month which you can spend to pay for goods and services. At the end of each month you receive a statement that itemizes all your purchases and you can choose to pay off the whole lot or just some of it. Provided you meet the minimum payments you can stay in debt as long as you like and pay a vastly inflated rate of interest for the privilege.

This is not an exaggeration, nor is it puritanical. Credit card companies – even the most respectable – are just loan companies under a different guise. Their sole purpose in life is to tempt you into debt and to make money by charging well above the rates of interest you could get if you arranged a simple bank loan.

So it's from a finance company.
So, it's better than no letter at all!
So they want the third payment on the Plymouth.

[dropping each letter on the floor in turn]

So they want
the fourth ... the fifth ...
the sixth ... the seventh ...

So they want the Plymouth.

Shapiro, *Stalag 17* (1953)

Having said that, few people would be without their credit card. It saves you budgeting on a daily or weekly basis and is extremely convenient, particularly where you want to make purchases by telephone or via the Internet.

Mean money

Bear in mind that nobody is obliged to give you credit and if you are turned down the company may have consulted a credit reference agency, which keeps records of people who do not pay their debts.

Which type of card?

The card you choose should be suitable for your spending habits. If you intend to pay in full every month and use the card just for convenience then the annual percentage rate of interest charged (APR) is pretty irrelevant. In this case you should look for a card that has no annual charge and offers as long as possible to pay your bill. Some of the new entrants from the USA are good value.

The big four banks – Barclays, Lloyds TSB, Midland and NatWest – still dominate the market with a 60-per-cent share – despite the fact that they tend to charge a fairly high APR and continue to make a one-off annual fee.

Most people intend to pay their bills every month but once or twice a year slip up and get caught. If you fit this description, you need a card that offers a competitive rate of interest.

Perks

Due to the increased competition, most cards offer some sort of perks – for example travel accident insurance and insurance against loss or damage of items you purchase with the card. Other cards offer points that you can trade for store vouchers or goods. Goldfish credit cards allow you to redeem points for money off your gas bill, TV licence and telephone bills.

Store cards

Most major stores or high-street chains offer a credit card that works just like any other except you can only use it to purchase from that particular store or range of stores. It is debatable whether such cards are of any real value – much depends on the added convenience the card gives you. For example, you may get a discount on purchases and be allowed early access to sale items.

So, what is the downside? The obvious drawback is that you will probably end up spending more than you would normally do, simply because you have a card. Also, bear in mind that if you build up credit on a store card you are not using your main credit card and earning points or airmiles or whatever you have opted for.

There are no hard and fast rules. Just ask yourself if you really want to be bothered with the paperwork and monthly bills from every shop you ever use. Finally, remember that if you are persuaded to sign up during the summer sales and regret the decision, you can pay off the debt and cancel the card.

Donation cards

Several leading charities, including Amnesty International, Comic Relief, Oxfam, Save the Children, and Unicef, offer their own credit card. Most will make an initial donation of £5 or £10 to the relevant charity or affinity group as soon as you join. After that they donate anything between 0.25 percent and 0.5 percent of all purchases made with the card.

Whether or not you go for this type of card is very much down to your principles. Do make sure, however, that the card isn't more expensive than cards from mainstream issuers. If it is, you would be better off just making a modest monthly donation by standing order to your favourite charity. If you do this by deed of covenant the charity can also claim back the tax you have paid, which makes it a very efficient way of giving.

At first I found it hard to believe that my father was Japanese, and that I was part-Japanese. But that would explain why I've always had these strange, non-American urges to work very hard, save money and live without credit cards.

Toxic Avenger, *Toxic Avenger, Part II* (1989).

The annual percentage rate

The annual percentage rate of charge (APR) is supposed to be a standard way of working out all the different methods credit-card issuers and other lenders use to calculate the interest you pay on a loan. It should take into account the size, number and frequency of the payments and any other built-in charges. The idea – and it's a good one – is that you should be able to compare all the different rates, like for like, in order to make an informed choice over which is the best for your circumstances.

One problem with the APR that was spotted by the Consumers' Association is that some credit-card issuers charge interest from the day the purchase is noted on your account. Others charge from the date it appears on your statement, which clearly is cheaper and may make an apparently less favourable APR come out tops.

It's up to you whether you want to go into the real nitty gritty of APRs. Frankly, you would be better off just repaying your balance every month and bypassing the APR minefield altogether.

Mean money
If you intend to pay in full every month and use the card just for convenience then the annual percentage rate of interest charged (APR) is pretty irrelevant.

One point you should check though is the way your card issuer deals with cash withdrawals. Generally you should avoid drawing cash on credit because this is likely to be far more expensive than an authorized overdraft from your bank. Most card issuers charge a fixed percentage for cash withdrawals and if you don't repay the withdrawal in full after the next statement you will pay interest as well.

Mean money
Provided you meet the minimum payments you can stay in debt as long as you like and pay a vastly inflated rate of interest for the privilege.

Troubleshooting

If you have a credit problem or think there is a problem with a credit agreement you have signed, seek advice from the Citizens Advice Bureau or your local trading standards department. Don't go to a licensed credit broker – they earn up to £1,000 in commission for 'consolidating' your debts and you will pay through the nose.

Bear in mind that if you owe money the creditor is entitled to try to get you to repay it. However, he or she must not put you under undue pressure – for example by contacting your employer or banging on your front door every five minutes.

Summary

- Consider whether you want an affinity group card through which you will make a modest donation – typically 0.25 per cent of the purchase price – to your favourite charity, trade union, political party whenever you use your card. However, don't sign up unless the card is otherwise competitive.

- Shop around for cards that charge less punitive rates if you do not manage to pay off your balance occasionally. Check the annual percentage rate (APR) and make sure you are comparing like with like.

- If you plan to pay the balance every month, look for a company that does not make an annual charge, or will waive the charge after a certain level of use.

- Set yourself a monthly limit for purchases.

- Pay off the balance each month whenever possible.

- If you build up a debt you cannot repay over the short term, consider taking out a lower interest bank loan to pay it off. Alternatively, some card issuers offer low introductory rates of interest for debt transfer – but for a limited period only, typically six months.

Further information

For comparisons between credit and debit card
issuers, *see Moneyfacts* (page 30).
National Debtline (for free confidential advice) 10
am–4 pm Monday and Thursday, 2 pm to 7 pm
Tuesday and Wednesday: 0121 359 8501.
National Association of Citizens Advice Bureaux: 020
7833 2181.
Consumer Credit Counselling Service: 0113 234
2202.

Work is a
four-
letter word

Make enough money
and everything **else** will
follow. **Quote me.**
That's a **fishism**.

Richard Fish, *Ally McBeal* (1997)

[Still from *The Rebel*, Canal+Image UK Ltd]

chapter 4

My brilliant career

Well, here goes. I hope I get the job. Of course, with my spider-power I could get all the money I'd ever need, but that wouldn't be honest. I'm a crime fighter now.

Peter Parker/Spiderman,
Spider-Man (1967)

After reading this chapter you will:

- want to be a high-flyer in a major financial institution;

- want to marry someone who is a high-flyer in a major financial institution;

- return the luncheon vouchers and demand a stock option.

It's Wednesday morning and it feels like a Monday. In half an hour you've got yet another meeting with the enthusiastic new chief executive who's just flown in from the USA. He has a stock option the size of a planet, and an ego to match.

The telephone rings. It's the recruitment consultant and he wants a quiet word. He gets it. On offer is a job with more money and prestige than your present position. So, is it one in the eye for the boss and free drinks all round at the Slug and Lettuce?

Perhaps, but first a word of caution. Changing jobs is a risky business. You've seen the headline salary but that's only part of the story. The rest of the package can add anything from 20 to 100 per cent of the value of the salary to the overall figure. A £30k salary from a small company that offers nothing else can be worth a lot less than a £25k salary with a blue-chip company that offers everything from a first-class pension and stock-option scheme, to company car, disability and life cover.

Your benefit shopping list

This chapter is not going to help you get a job. What it will do is help you judge the value of your remuneration package. Equally important, if you are thinking of becoming self-employed, you need to be aware of how much it will cost you to replace these benefits through private insurance and investments (*see* Sections 4 and 5).

So, before you look at those headline salaries, consider how much you want or need the other benefits.

The basics

Pension

A traditional scheme aims to provide a tax-free cash lump sum and up to two-thirds of final salary as a retirement income. A spouse's pension is also paid if you die. Employees tend to contribute about 5–6 per cent of salary, while employers contribute on your behalf a further 10–12 per cent. Your contributions benefit from full tax relief (*see* Chapter 14).

Mean money

Changing jobs is a risky business. You've seen the headline salary but that's only part of the story. The rest of the package can add anything from 20–100 per cent of the value of the salary to the overall figure.

Okay, I'll tell you **this much.** The world runs on money. Everybody walks around with this **invisible number** in their heads. You **hit** the figure close enough, the penny drops, you **own** the man.

Ray, *Stingray* (1986)

Life assurance

This is a tax-free cash lump sum that is paid to your dependants if you die. The maximum permitted by Inland Revenue is four times annual salary. Most employers pay between three and four times salary (*see* Chapter 16).

Disability insurance

Permanent health insurance (PHI) pays a replacement income until retirement if you are too ill to work. Two-thirds of salary index linked is typical.

The big extras

Company car

The employer usually pays for the purchase price, insurance, repairs and running costs. In some cases your employer might also pay for petrol for private use. The annual value might be anything from £10,000 to £20,000. Due to the less favourable tax treatment of company cars in recent years, some employers offer the cash equivalent instead.

Annual bonus

This can be anything from 15–20 per cent of salary for a middle manager in manufacturing, rising to 100 per cent for senior people in financial institutions.

Share schemes

There are several ways in which your employer can offer you the opportunity to buy shares in the company at lower than market value. You may be able to avoid income tax on what is effectively a benefit in kind (the difference between the reduced price and the market price is regarded as a type of payment from your employer) if the offer is part of an Inland-Revenue-approved share-option scheme.

Stock options

This is a type of golden handcuff for the long-term dedicated senior manager. The terms can be magnificent, but only if you are committed to staying put and only if the company's performance is good. Depending on market conditions and the company's progress, a three-year option is likely to add about 50–100 per cent to your annual salary – more for very senior people.

But these glittering prizes are not all that they seem. In fact in the UK it can be hard to put a value on stock options because, under corporate governance rules, the company must meet specific growth targets before the schemes can pay out.

There are two types of directors' share remuneration and it is important to understand the difference:

- *stock options* offer the right to buy a share at a fixed price in the future, usually after three years and then annually – the option only has a value if the share price goes up during the initial three years and continues to rise each year;

- *restricted shares* are free, so whatever the share price they have a value.

The bigger the stock option the more important it is to seek advice on its potential value. Some companies are looking for real

Mean money
A traditional pension scheme aims to provide a tax-free cash lump sum and up to two-thirds of final salary as a retirement income. Employers typically pay 10–12 per cent of salary towards this benefit.

entrepreneurs. If you join a start-up e-commerce company, for example, you may have to take an initial cut in salary, but the stock option can be extraordinarily valuable if the company is successful.

When you change jobs you may find that the stock-option scheme rules are usually set in stone, but you may be able to negotiate entry terms and receive compensation for the embedded value of the option in your existing scheme.

Top tips for the negotiating table

- Before agreeing on a renumeration package, ask: what are the contract terms? Many companies only offer a 12-month rolling contract.

- What is the £ value of the benefits offered? A high salary may not compensate for the loss of other important benefits if you currently have a good pension and stock-option scheme.

- How is your pension affected by the move? The salary on which it is based may be restricted so you need to be compensated. Seek actuarial advice.

- Do you have a stock option or are you being offered the more valuable restricted shares?

- How does the potential annual value compare with your current package? Can you get compensation for the embedded value of your existing options?

- How is the annual bonus calculated? Check the level of discretionary bonuses in recent years. Can you get a guarantee for the first year?

- Does the job involve overseas assignments and if so will you be compensated in full for changes in the standard of living?

To help you put a cash value on the most valuable items in your benefits package, take a look at the total compensation package of two employees in Table 4.1.

Table 4.1 What's your price tag?

PROFILE: Middle manager, age 25	
Salary (per annum)	£25,000 per annum
Bonus (15 per cent of salary)	£3,750
Employer's contribution to pension	£2,500
Life assurance (cost of 4 times salary protection)	£100
Income protection	£300
Private medical insurance for family (if applicable)	£1,000
Company car	£7,500
Total value of salary and benefits package	£40,150

Notes: Pension is based on a sixtieths scheme and an employer's contribution of roughly 10 per cent of salary; company car retail purchase price £18,750.

PROFILE: Middle manager, age 30, married with a non-working wife and two small children	
Salary (per annum)	£35,000 per annum
Bonus (15 per cent of salary)	£5,250
Pension	£3,500
Life assurance (Cost of 4 times salary protection)	£100
Income protection	£300
Private medical insurance	£1,000
Company car	£7,500
Stock option	up to 50% annual salary
Total value of salary and benefits package	£52,650 plus stock option

Notes: Pension is based on a sixtieths scheme and an employer's contribution of roughly 10 per cent of salary; company car retail purchase price £18,750; the value of the company share scheme is dependent on market movements.

Overseas secondments

So, your boss is packing you off to South America for three years to develop those challenging overseas subsidiaries. Do you:

- jump for joy?
- develop a nervous rash?
- wonder if your spouse will view this as grounds for divorce?

Whether you greet your overseas assignment with delight or grim acceptance, you need to make sure you are being paid the going rate – and this includes many peripherals in addition to your cash remuneration. In fact in some of the toughest locations in the world it can cost a company nine times more to relocate an expatriate and his or her family than to hire a local.

The big multinationals tend to have formal benefits and pay structures for expatriates, so there may not be much room for negotiation. However, with many employers the value of your package will be directly linked to your bargaining skills.

Clearly the benefits package will depend on how badly the company wants you for the assignment. If you volunteer for a secondment in Brussels as a career move, do not expect the same red-carpet treatment the company might offer a key executive whom they want to ship off to a volcanic island inhabited by cannibals who are in the throes of a revolution.

Expat compensation

Before you accept a secondment overseas, make sure your salary and employee benefits package compensates you for the stress and domestic upheavals.

You want to compare brainpans. I won the Westinghouse prize when I was 12, big deal. Published at 19, so what. I got a double doctorate from MIT at 22, Chemistry and Geology. I taught at Princeton for two and a half years. Why do I do *this*? Because the money's good, the scenery changes and they let me use explosives.

Rockhound, *Armageddon* (1998)

- Taxation – get the company to pay the tax on your benefits or at least guarantee that you pay no more tax than at present on your UK package.

- Make sure that your current position is secure for when you return (50 per cent of international companies do not offer this guarantee).

- Check that your local salary is adjusted in line with a recognized cost-of-living index – but remember, the adjustment may be zero or even negative.

An estimated 38 per cent of kidnap victims are company employees, according to AIG, part of the international insurer American International Group. Check security arrangements very carefully if you are going to Latin America, the Philippines, South Africa, Yemen, Nigeria and Somalia. Serious kidnapping problems are also emerging in Russia and the Commonwealth of Independent States, AIG reports.

Before travelling to these regions you need clear instructions on where the no-go areas are and how to avoid attracting attention. In certain parts of the world you can appear ostentatiously wealthy by wearing smart glasses or carrying a laptop. In some locations you might need a driver or bodyguard.

International consultant William M. Mercer explained how culture shock led to a failed assignment to South Africa, which lasted just six months. Security problems were the most serious concern:

> The expatriate found that he could not stop at red traffic lights at night, that people live behind electric fences, that there are panic buttons in the home to alert guards, that people openly carry guns while going about their everyday lives, that car doors must be locked and windows wound up at all times – the list is endless. This was a big adjustment to make for someone moving from London to Johannesburg where you can't even go for a Sunday stroll in the park.

> **Mean money**
> The annual bonus can be anything from 15–20 per cent of salary for a middle manager in manufacturing, rising to 100 per cent for senior people in financial institutions.

- Often companies will pay a premium for additional responsibility or as an incentive to move. Typically this could be 5 per cent for a secondment in another continent, 5 per cent for a different language, and 5 per cent for a major change in culture.

- If you are going to a tough location – for example Eastern Europe, the Middle East, or Africa – you should also receive a hardship premium on top of the job premium. This could be worth up to 50 per cent of salary.

- Find out if you qualify for 'rest and relaxation' benefits. For example if you are sent to a dry state your employer may pay to transport you to a more 'relaxing' environment at regular intervals.

- Your pension is important. Will you be retained in the UK scheme and given a guarantee not to be worse off when you return? Seek advice if you have a personal pension or pay free-standing additional voluntary contributions. As a non-resident

you will not be able to continue investing in these schemes. (For more details on your pension, *see* Chapters 14 and 15.)

- Share options are a major issue for executives. Seek professional advice before exercising your rights to avoid double taxation. A double tax bill (that is a bill in the UK and in your country of secondment) would not be covered by your employer's tax protection programme because it is classed as personal income.

- Your employer may pay for your accommodation, but be prepared to make a contribution.

- What about a company car? If this is not a standard benefit in the country of assignment, for example in the USA, ask for compensation.

- Don't budge without international private medical insurance for the whole family, including emergency repatriation if the standard of local care is poor.

- Your employer should pay for private education for your children at home or locally, depending on location.

- Check security thoroughly. Expats in Moscow, for example, may need a driver/bodyguard.

- Remember, financial compensation will not help you and your family to adapt to a very different local culture. Depending on location you should consider insisting on a pre-departure cultural briefing for you and your partner (*see* Further information on page 53).

- Insist on free private use of the Internet to keep in touch with friends and family.

Mean money

The big multinationals tend to have formal benefits and pay structures for expatriates' pay and benefits packages, so there may not be much room for negotiation. However, with many employers the value of your package will be directly linked to your bargaining skills.

International assignments formula

If you want to know what the going rate is for your assignment, your best bet is to check what the big multinationals offer. One FTSE-100 company, which has formal employee benefits package for international assignments, offers:

- *Remuneration*: based on local salaries, which may be supplemented in local currency. On top of this, a 'home element' net of tax is paid in most countries. This is designed to cover home commitments, holidays and savings.

- *A bonus*: paid at the end of the assignment. This varies according to the level of perceived hardship in the country. For example assignees to Nigeria and Bangladesh receive 30 per cent of their home salary net of tax. In other countries this might be just 5 per cent.

Other elements of financial support include:

- *Education for your children* (if applicable): either 80 per cent of boarding school fees plus two trips to visit parents, or 100 per cent of overseas school fees.

- *Housing*: employees usually pay 12.5 per cent of local salary towards housing but in some cases the company may cover the whole bill. It also pays a subsidy to cover any expenses at home – for example council tax, water rates, repairs and maintenance, and any gaps between the cost of the mortgage and the rent received.

- *A disturbance allowance*: one month's salary tax free.

- *Travel*: one visit home per annum.

- *A rest and recreation allowance*: this exists only in countries that have a very high level of hardship.

- *Transport*: whatever is appropriate to the local environment.

- *Holidays*: between five and six weeks.

The company commented: 'It is clear to us that whole families have a stake in an international move and increasingly we provide assistance in job hunting for the spouse and in providing flexible family care, for example.'

Certainly a good employer will help you and your family prepare for the assignment. This might include a four-week one-to-one language tuition course, a pre-departure briefing at a specialist cultural briefing centre and a visit to the country of assignment for the employee and spouse.

Summary

- Don't just look at the salary – consider the value of the other benefits as well.
- Pensions, life assurance and disability insurance are the chief benefits.
- Major extras include a company car, the annual bonus and a stock option.
- Remember, valuable stock options will tie you to the company for a considerable time.
- If you are asked to move overseas, work through the checklist here to make sure you are being paid the going rate.
- Find out if your job is guaranteed on your return.

Further information

The Centre for International Briefings, based at Farnham Castle in Surrey, is used by many multinationals for pre-secondment briefings for employees and their families. The centre covers over 150 countries and can offer tuition in virtually any language (01252 721194; www.cibfarnham.com).

chapter 5

The company of wolves: the new entrepreneurs

You don't go **wheelin 'n dealin** for money. You do it for **fun**. Money's just the way you keep score.

Henry Tycoon,
The Wheeler Dealers (1963)

After reading this chapter you will:

- knit yourself a jumper like Richard Branson's;

- sell your soul to the Devil for a business loan;

- decide there's a lot to be said for being a pen-pusher in the civil service.

Steady jobs for life are history. These days five years shows an uncalled-for commitment to one company unless you are shooting up the ranks so fast you need oxygen.

There is an alternative. If you fancy doing your own thing, either as a sole trader or going into business with friends, family or like-minded colleagues, there are some fantastic opportunities. There are also some unbelievably deep pitfalls.

About 320,000 people become self-employed and start up small businesses in the UK each year. Over two-thirds of these do not have any previous experience of running a small firm. A third of these need external funding, according to research from Barclays Bank. Others require additional funding to develop and expand an existing business. Whichever stage you are at, this chapter will help start you off in the right direction.

Banks are the main source of loans. However, there is a wide range of other sources of finance and this chapter looks in particular at the schemes targeted at 'young people' (generally 30 and under), then outlines some of the help and information services available.

One of the best guides to starting your own business is free and available from the Department of Trade and Industry (DTI): *Small firms: Financing your business*. Details for this and other information sources and organizations mentioned in this chapter are provided on page 67.

Before seeking funding, talk to your local Business Link, and your accountant. The Business Link and Department for Education and Employment (DfEE) also offer advice on a range of subjects including employment law and training.

Why are you going into business?

Your reason for being in business in the first place is the single most important factor in determining what type of finance is suitable. You may be in business to provide for your family, to be your own boss, because you cannot find another job, to make lots of money, or because you are teeming with ideas and no one company can contain you.

Whatever your reason, it is important to recognize how it will affect your attitude to risk and to whether or not you feel comfortable handing over some of the control to investors.

Are you an entrepreneur?

If your chief aim in business is to provide a low-risk way of looking after your family or to provide yourself with a steady source of income that you cannot find elsewhere, then you had better stick to the traditional methods of raising finance, such as a bank overdraft or loan.

If, on the other hand, you recognize the characteristics in yourself listed in box 5.1, you

Mean money
Your reason for being in business in the first place is the single most important factor in determining what type of finance is suitable.

may have the key entrepreneurial attributes that make your business suitable for raising venture capital (*see* page 58).

Structures for business

Businesses are either unincorporated – like sole traders and partnerships – or they are incorporated limited companies. The distinction affects the way you can raise money:

• *Unincorporated businesses*: sole traders and partnerships are only able to raise additional capital from their own resources by allowing new partners to buy into the business.

• *Incorporated limited companies*: these businesses are able to raise equity by issuing shares. However, there are many constraints on this type of company – for example you have to submit accounts to the Registrar of Companies and recognize the rights of shareholders.

How many of these key entrepreneurial attributes do you have?

- drive and energy
- the ability to learn from others
- the ability to respond to what the market wants
- tenacity and courage
- hunger for success
- self-confidence
- willingness to assess opportunities and to take a calculated risk
- the ability to motivate other people to work productively for you
- the ability to set high achievable goals
- the belief in your ability to control your own destiny
- a long-term view of where your business is going
- readiness to learn from your mistakes and setbacks
- the ability to be competitive with good self-discipline.

Source: DTI

Why do you need money?

This is not a daft question. In order to convince a lender you are trustworthy you will need to demonstrate that you have thought very carefully about how much money you need and which aspects of your business it will assist. For example do you need it to buy equipment or to pay for project development costs?

Consider these facts and figures provided by Barclays Bank:

- the average cost of setting up in business is about £18,000 – typically one-third of this is funded externally;
- external funding is primarily used to finance business premises (29 per cent) and stock (21 per cent) – it is rarely used for wages or recruitment;

- banks are the main source of external finance for both start-up businesses (72 per cent) and established businesses (86 per cent) – friends and families are an important secondary source;

- only one in five firms investigates whether it is eligible for government or EU grants.

I've learned something too. Selling out is sweet because you get to make a lot of money and don't have to hang around with poor asses like you guys. Screw you guys, I'm going home.

Cartman, *South Park* (1997)

In general you can expect to borrow between £500 and £25,000. You are likely to be asked to repay in monthly instalments over a term of between one and ten years. If this a start-up business, you may be able to negotiate an interest-and-capital-repayment holiday for up to six months to tide you over the crucial first months, when cashflow can be a problem.

The average time for a small business to raise finance varies considerably. Barclays suggests this can be anything from one week to one month but this is for fairly straightforward loans. If you are after venture capital, for example, you should allow four to seven months – longer if you do not yet have a business plan.

Financing your business

The main sources of finance for businesses are banks and similar financial institutions, although the government does provide some help, particularly in areas where it is trying to increase employment and attract new business.

How you raise money will depend on your specific needs, the amount required and, frankly, sheer availability. Discuss this with your accountant before approaching any lenders.

Equity capital

Raising equity capital involves selling a share of your company to a venture capital company or an informal investor (sometimes known as a business angel). Venture capital companies are the main providers of equity finance for new companies, but their preference for larger investments makes them rather inaccessible for small start-ups, although it is still worth checking the British Venture Capital Association (BVCA) website (*see* page 68).

Mean money

If this is a start-up business, you may be able to negotiate with your lender an interest-and-capital repayment holiday for up to six months to tide you over the crucial first months, when cashflow can be a problem.

Business angels

Business angels are private individuals, usually with a business background, who are willing to invest in small businesses in return for an equity stake. Generally they are able and keen to offer the benefits of their own management experience.

Several organizations have grouped together under the umbrella of the Business Angels Network to match businesses seeking equity finance with potential investors. Further information is available from the British Venture Capital Association and Business Links.

Loans

Probably the best starting point for loans is your local bank if you have a good track record there. However, you should also check the market for top borrowing rates. An excellent source of information is *Business Moneyfacts*, details of which are on page 30.

The guidelines here about availability of finance and the time it takes to secure a loan are averages only. In general banks are much more willing to lend to older people with a business track record than to a young entrepreneur. Even more good reason to do your homework and rehearse presentation well!

It may be tempting to approach your friends and your family for finance, but do be aware of the drawbacks. The bank will set its terms and conditions and stick to them. If you get into trouble you will know in advance at exactly which point the bank will start to pester you and what action you will be required to take.

Friends and family may also have a tendency to interfere – if things do go wrong, your personal as well as your professional peace of mind is at risk. Having said that, family businesses are among the robust in the economy.

Look at all available sources of finance. Loan finance normally requires regular payments of capital and interest. Leasing and hire purchase may be another way of financing some of your business requirements.

How to present your case

Barclays Bank has put together a good formula for making an effective presentation, which it calls 'CAMPARI':

- *Character*: present yourself positively and demonstrate your commitment and enthusiasm for your business. Bank managers place a great deal of importance on these qualities when assessing proposals.

- *Ability*: demonstrate that you have the appropriate experience, training and drive to plan and run your business effectively. An up-to-date copy of your CV will help here.

- *Management*: show that you have the ability to produce up-to-date and accurate financial information to demonstrate your control over the business.

Mean money

Look at all available sources of finance. Loan finance normally requires regular payments of capital and interest. Leasing and hire purchase may be another way of financing some of your business requirements.

- *Purpose*: explain in detail your reason for seeking bank funding. This will enable the bank to identify the right loan package for your needs if it decides to help you. It will also enable the bank to calculate the level of risk it is taking in lending you money. This in turn will affect the rate of interest it offers and the terms and conditions.

- *Amount*: be precise and show how you have calculated the size of loan you need. If you borrow too much this will add to your costs. Do, however, make an allowance for contingencies. If you ask for too little, you may have to return to the bank at a later date.

- *Repayment*: be clear about the sources of repayment. Develop cashflow and budget forecasts that show accurately how you expect the business to develop over the term of the loan. Outline the sources from which repayments will be met.

- *Insurance*: protect yourself and your business. The bank will want to know how you will meet repayments if your business experiences cashflow problems. You may need to offer some sort of security. You should also consider whether you need to take out appropriate insurance to protect the repayment of the loan in case you are unable to meet the cost from normal trade due to accident, illness (or even death!). Key personnel should be covered as well as yourself.

Barclays commented:

Bank managers look first and foremost at the character, ability and experience of the business owner and the cash generating capacity of the business itself. In this respect it is essential to stress the importance of proper planning and forecasting before any meeting with the bank manager.

Your business plan

Your business plan needs to present the key facts to the lender or investor in a clear and concise fashion. You need to set out where you are going and how you are going to get there. The plan, therefore, will combine your own objectives and the potential of your business (*see* box 5.2). As an owner, the DTI suggests you should set out:

- what you want out of the business;
- when you want to realize your wealth (that is, sell up);
- your strengths and weaknesses.

Both lenders and equity investors will need to be convinced about the viability of the business. This depends initially on two factors – sales and management. So, when you approach a source of funding or investment, your priority is to prove that there is a market for the product or service and that the management team is sufficiently experienced and capable of identifying problems and devising solutions to steer a successful path.

**box 5.2
Business
plan outline**

- *Executive summary*
- *The business*: history, current status
- *Products*: description, regulatory requirements, research and development
- *Production process*: techniques, location, supplier, capacity
- *Sales and marketing*: market size, competition, sales analysis by product and customer marketing techniques
- *Management and organization*: management team with full CVs, organization chart, remuneration policies
- *Financial information*: historical results (if relevant), profit and cashflow projections, sensitivity (e.g. to changing interest rates), financing requirements
- *The future*: future prospects, exit routes for the investor

How to sell your plan

The providers of loans and equity will have different priorities and motives in assessing a business plan.

Providers of equity are looking for a significant capital gain to justify their risk, and a built-in exit route. Lenders are not seeking to make such large returns, nor will they accept such a high level of risk as an equity investor. However, since their aim is to minimize losses, they may ask you to provide adequate security for the loan.

Restrict circulation to just a few potential sources of finance. With each rejection (and there may be many of these!) revise your plan to reflect what you have learned.

The four key steps suggested by the DTI are:

- sell the idea on paper – convey what it is that makes the project exciting in the minimum number of words and ensure your presentation is eye catching;
- consult professional advisers who have a knowledge of financiers;
- follow up with a telephone call and arrange a meeting at which you, the management, can sell the idea and prove your ability;
- after the meeting consider amending the plan to take account of the financier's comments.

Back home **everyone** said I didn't have **any talent**. They might **be saying** the **same thing** over here, but it **sounds better** in **French**.

Jerry Mulligan, *An American President* (1951)

Business support

Your first port of call for most business enquiries is your nearest Business Link service. These are local partnerships that bring together the business support services of the DTI, Training and Enterprise Councils, Chambers of Commerce, Enterprise Agencies, local authorities and other local bodies. There are 85 partnerships nationwide with some 240 outlets and 650 advisers.

These centres can help with a wide range of issues, including advice for start-up businesses, training, finance packaging, design, export, marketing, and access to other specialist businesses. For details of the Business Link Signpost Line, the Scottish Business Shops, the Northern Ireland Local Enterprise Development Unit (LEDU) and the Business Link Connect service in Wales, *see* page 67.

You can also visit the Business Link website for information on:

- business and market research
- sources of grants and finance
- company and product sourcing
- Companies House and credit information.

Small firms loan guarantee scheme

The DTI's small firms loan guarantee scheme (SFLGS) provides a government guarantee for loans approved by lenders. Loans are made to firms or individuals who are unable to raise conventional finance due to the lack of a track record or the high-risk nature of the proposed business. The guarantee generally covers 70 per cent of the outstanding loan, rising to 85 per cent for established businesses that have been trading for two years or more. Typical loans covered range from £5,000 up to £100,000 (£200,000 for established businesses), which must be repaid over a period of two to 10 years.

Government development areas

The government provides discretionary grants if you are brave enough to set up business in what are euphemistically called 'assisted areas'. Projects must either create new jobs or safeguard existing ones to qualify. Check out Regional Selective Assistance (RSA see page 68).

Other sources of help

- *The Prince's Youth Business Trust* provides business counselling for the under-25s who want to start their own business. In particular it can provide grants and low-interest loans to people aged 18–30 in England and 18–25 in Scotland who are not able to raise the finance through more traditional channels.

- *Livewire* is sponsored by the oil and chemicals company Shell UK Ltd and offers advice and assistance for business start-ups for entrepreneurs aged 16–29. If you make an enquiry you will automatically receive a free booklet that will help you to think through the process of starting your own business, provide details of a local business adviser and a fact sheet on your business idea. Livewire also holds an annual competition to reward the achievements of young people new to business.

- *The Enterprise Zone* provides an Internet-based information service to business.

- *Trade associations*, which represent the interests of specialist industries or groups of traders, can be a valuable source of information. Good reference libraries should stock the *Directory of British Associations* which lists all the trade associations.

- *The Agricultural Development and Advisory Services (ADAS)* provides research-based technical and business information on prospects in agriculture. Together with Business Link, among others, ADAS provides diagnostic, planning and feasibility studies to farms and farm-based businesses in certain areas.

- *Professional help*: local accountants are well geared towards helping the small business (look for them in *Yellow Pages*), while many solicitors participate in the 'Lawyers for Your Business' scheme which offers a free legal consultation or legal health-check if you are about to set up your own business (*see* page 68 for the website).

- *Franchising*: one option for budding entrepreneurs is to buy a franchise or to turn an existing business into a franchise operation. There is a dedicated organization for help with franchising – the British Franchise Association (*see* page 68). It is also worth getting copies of two DTI Small Firms Publications: *Buying a Franchise* and *Franchising Your Business*.

State-run training and support schemes

If you have been unemployed for more than six months you may qualify for work-based training and receive training and financial support to help you set up in self-employment. Information is available through your local jobcentre.

You may also qualify for Business Enterprise assistance if you live or are prepared to work in a designated area where the government is trying to promote employment. This scheme offers:

- training to develop a business plan
- grants for equipment
- rehearsal trading and mentoring.

Mean money

The government provides discretionary grants if you are brave enough to set up business in what are euphemistically called 'assisted areas'. Projects must either create new jobs or safeguard existing ones to qualify.

Small firms training loans

The DfEE sponsors a scheme that provides training loans to small firms through eight major banks: Barclays, Midland, Lloyds TSB, NatWest, Bank of Scotland, Clydesdale, Co-operative and the Royal Bank of Scotland. The scheme helps businesses with up to 50 employees pay for vocational training or education by offering loans on deferred repayment terms.

You can borrow up to £125,000 of help towards consultancy advice on training issues. In most cases applications must be endorsed by the local TEC/LEC (Training Education Council/Local Education Council) before they are submitted to the bank.

You can get an information pack and application form by calling the freefone number on page 68.

Patent Office

It is important to protect a new business idea, invention or logo through the Patent Office. Contact the office for advice on patents, designs, trade marks and copyright.

Information technology

The Information Society Initiative (ISI) 'Programme for Business' has established a network of local support centres that offer advice and guidance on the benefits and use of information and communications technology by business. Some centres offer access to facilities like video conferencing and may provide training or point you in the right direction for local expertise. ISI also produces a range of helpful brochures.

The Software Business Network is an Internet-based information service for young software companies. It provides support in marketing, management and access to capital, among other services

A good starting point for Internet sites for business is the Enterprise Zone Internet Service.

Employment law

This is a minefield but a good place to start is the Employers' helpline which gives advice on tax, national insurance contributions, statutory sick pay and value added tax (VAT) registration.

Summary

- Two-thirds of the 320,000 people who go into business each year do not have previous experience.
- You may decide to go into business to provide for your family, to be your own boss, because you cannot find another job, to make lots of money, or because you are teeming with ideas and no one company can contain you!
- The average cost of setting up in business is £18,000. Typically, one-third of this is funded externally.
- Banks are the main providers of business finance, but friends and family are also important sources.
- If you want to raise capital through equity you could try a venture capital company or a business angel – a private individual with an interest in new ventures.
- Prepare your business plan with care and market it on a virtually exclusive basis

Further information

Many of the figures in this chapter were provided by Barclays Bank Small Business Team. The Barclays website is at www.smallbusiness.barclays.co.uk

The Department of Trade and Industry publishes a range of useful booklets for people thinking of setting up or developing a small business. A good starter pack would be:

- *Small firms – financing your business* URN 98/805
- *Guide to help for small business* URN 98/942
- *Small firms publication list* URN 99/1058

To order, telephone 0870 1502 500 or e-mail dtipubs@echristian.co.uk. You should also check out the DTI publications website on www.dti.gov.uk/publications/sme

Business Moneyfacts: 01603 476476

Business Link

Business Link: www.businesslink.co.uk
Business Link Signpost Line: 0345 567765
Business Link Connect Wales: 0345 969798 (e-mail: www.bc.wales.org.uk)
Northern Ireland Local Enterprise Development Unit (LEDU): 028 9049 1031

Business support services

Agricultural Development and Advisory Services
(ADAS): 01865 842742 (www.adas.co.uk)
British Franchise Association: 01491 578049/50
(www.british-franchise.org.uk)
Companies House: 029 2038 0801
Employment Zones: 020 7925 5958
(www.dfee.gov.uk)
English Tourist Board: 020 8846 9000
The Enterprise Zone: www.enterprisezone.org.uk
Federation of Small Businesses: www.fsb.co.uk
Highlands and Islands Enterprise: 01463 234171
Lawyers for Your Business: 020 7405 9075
(www.lfyb.lawsociety.org.uk)
Livewire (start-up awards): 0191 261 5584
Livewire Hotline for information and advice: 0345
573252 (www.shell-livewire.org)
Northern Ireland Tourist Board: 028 9023 1221
The Patent Office: www.patent.gov.uk
The Prince's Scottish Youth Business Trust: 0141 248
4999
The Prince's Youth Business Trust: 020 7543 1234
Scottish Business Shops – Lowlands: freefone 0800
787878
Scottish Enterprise: 0141 248 2700
Wales Tourist Board: 029 2049 9909

Finance

British Venture Capital Association (BVCA): 020
7240 3846 (www.brainstorm.co.uk/BVCA)
Regional Selective Assistance (RSA) in England:
contact Business Link
RSA in Scotland: 0141 242 5675/5676
RSA in Wales: 029 2082 3216
Small Firms Loan Guarantee Scheme: 0114 259
7308/9
Small firms training loans: freefone 0800 132660

Information technology

Information Society Initiative: www.isi.gov.uk
Enterprise Zone Internet Service:
www.enterprisezone.org.uk
Software Business Network: 020 7395 6700

Employment

Employers' helpline: 0345 143143

Insolvency

The DTI's insolvency service is at
www.open.gov.uk/insolv_s/insolvhm.htm

chapter 6

Big brother is watching

Are you **telling me** you can **speak** six languages and **fly** a jetliner but you don't know **how** to file a tax return? ... **It's never** come up? ... Does this have to happen right **now?** ... No, that's a 'W-2'. 'WW2' was the Second World War.

Steve Arlo, *Zero Effect* (1998)

After reading this chapter you will:

- feel more sympathy for obscenely rich tax exiles;

- understand why Mick Jagger, the bad boy of rock, knows so much about the UK tax treatment of overseas employment;

- wish you were a rock star rather than a tax inspector.

What is tax?

No one likes paying tax and you really don't want to have to pay any more than is absolutely necessary. On the other hand, if you evade paying tax you will commit a criminal offence and you could be fined or, in extreme cases, end up in the nick. The Inland Revenue, which is responsible for collecting taxes, has heard all the excuses in the book – and a few more besides. So before you try it on, remember that all tax officials have undergone a triple humour, pity and empathy bypass.

Tax is the government's way of raising money to spend for the so-called 'common good'. There are many sources, including deductions from pay, from the profits of companies and businesses, from value added tax (VAT), road fuel, tobacco and alcohol duties.

The revenue raised is used to pay for a wide range of services and benefits, including health, education, defence, law and order, transport and social security. Cynics might argue that if you want a half-decent education or prompt health treatment you have to go privately, so you end up paying twice. They may have a point but it is not the purpose of this book to discuss the politics of welfare.

The government is not a good housekeeper and rarely sticks to its budget. If it raises £350 billion in revenue, it will probably spend £400 billion. To bridge the gap it issues government bonds, known as gilts, which are a type of IOU. Investors and financial institutions like to buy gilts, so there's no problem, provided we all continue to believe in the system and nobody points out that the emperor is stark naked.

When it comes to debt, the bigger you are the less it is a problem. However, students and other financial small fry receive little or no sympathy if they overspend. If you are broke, nobody is going to be interested in your IOUs so you will probably end up taking stuff to the pawnbrokers. It is cheering to note that as you get older, more cynical and, hopefully, richer, the less notice banks take if you overspend.

Income tax and national insurance

If you earn or receive income over a certain amount in any given tax year (6 April to 5 April) you have to pay income tax. The more you earn the more you pay. If you work for an employer, he or she is usually responsible for deducting the right amount and passing it on to the Inland Revenue. This is known as the pay-as-you earn (PAYE) system.

You also have to pay national insurance contributions (NICs) on earnings between a lower and upper threshold. The purists will howl at the over-simplification but you can regard NI as just another form of taxation. In

Buffy?
What's your sitch? You're acting like something from another tax bracket.

Kimberly, *Buffy the Vampire Slayer* (1992)

fact the days when NICs covered all the social security benefits are well past so the distinction is rather academic.

The Department of Social Security (DSS) will send you your NI number when you reach 16. It will look something like this: JX 34 25 16 B. You will need this for an extraordinarily large number of things, so keep a note of it in your diary or tattoo it on your knuckles.

NI thresholds and tax rates are set out in Table 6.1. These change at the beginning of every new tax year.

What is taxable?

The most common forms of taxable income are:

- pay and other earnings from regular or part-time employment. This includes tips, overtime and bonuses;
- profits from a business;
- interest from savings with a bank, building

Table 6.1 Main tax allowances and rates

See Chapter 13 for tips on how to make the most of these allowances and exemptions.

	2000–1 (£)
Allowances/exemptions	
Personal allowance under 65	4,385
Annual CGT exemption	7,200
Income tax	
Lower rate 10%	1,521
Basic rate 22%**	1,521–28,400
Higher rate 40%	over 28,400
Inheritance tax	
40%	over 234,000

Income tax is payable on earnings in excess of the relevant allowance.

Source: Inland Revenue

society and certain National Savings accounts (usually taxed at source unless you can prove you are a non-taxpayer);

- dividends from shares in companies;
- unemployment benefit.

Where is my tax office?

Take a map of the UK and find the furthest point from where you live or go to college. That is where your tax office will be. However the Inland Revenue has a Very Large Computer, which is supposed to be able to handle 64 million records, so if you need some information any tax office will be able to trace your details by checking under your NI number.

Your first job

Your first employer will give you a PAYE code based on your personal allowance. If your earnings are less than this allowance you will not pay tax.

When you change jobs your employer will give you a P45 form, which shows your PAYE code, your total earnings and how much tax you have paid since the start of the tax year. You must give this to your new employer or, if you are not going straight into another job, hand it in to your local benefit office. If you have claimed jobseeker's allowance (JSA) in the past you will already have a P45 from the jobcentre.

At the end of each year your employer will give you a P60 form, which shows how much you have earned and how much tax you have paid. The Revenue also gets a copy and should check the figures. If you have overpaid tax you will get a refund. Underpayments usually are deducted from your earnings during the following tax year.

When do you pay up?

If you are subject to PAYE, most of your tax will be paid through your employer's deductions. However, there may be other sources of income that you need to declare and pay tax on – for example any freelance

---

Mean money

The Inland Revenue, which is responsible for collecting taxes, has heard all the excuses in the book – and a few more besides. So before you try it on, remember that all tax officials have undergone a triple humour, pity and empathy bypass.

---

earnings and income from savings and investments. You will need to enter these details on the annual self-assessment form which you should receive in April (*see* page 75).

Students and tax

Student loans are not taxable, nor are certain other sources of cash (see Chapter 1). Full-time students don't have to pay tax on part-time or vacation work, provided you don't earn more than the single person's allowance (£4,385 in 2000–1). If you tell your employer you are a full-time student he or she will give you a P38(S) to complete.

Students on sandwich courses will be taxed on earnings during their year in industry and final year students will start to pay tax as soon as they start work.

Make sure you claim back any tax paid for part years in employment – for example if your sandwich year straddles two tax years or if you work for only part of a year before starting a course or after finishing one.

Self-employed and tax

There's more information on becoming self-employed and setting up your own business in Chapter 5. This section deals with the taxation issues. If you are unsure whether or not you are self-employed read the Inland Revenue leaflet IR56/NI39 *Employed or self-employed? A guide for tax and National Insurance.*

As soon as you start a business in a self-employed capacity you should inform the following authorities:

- the Inland Revenue (NI Contributions) Office;

- your local tax office;

- Customs and Excise: if your taxable turnover (total sales) is more than £50,000 in *any* 12-month rolling period you must register for VAT;

- your Jobcentre if you are registered with one (in Northern Ireland it would be the Training and Employment Agency).

If you get Inland Revenue leaflet CWL1 *Starting your own business?* you will find the relevant form for notifying these agencies.

Formal accounts?

At the very least the Inland Revenue will expect you to prepare an annual return of your business income and expenses. You may not need to prepare formal accounts but it is generally a good idea if you are having a serious bash at self-employment or starting your own business. Unless you have lots of time on your hands – and frankly if you are serious about making money you should be working around the clock – hire a qualified accountant to sort all of this stuff out for you. Accountants are not cheap but worth every

penny in terms of time saved and your credibility with the Inland Revenue.

Bear in mind that formal accounts are required for purposes other than just tax. If you want a business loan, for example, the bank is likely to want to see formal accounts to check your credibility and business acumen. The same is true if you want to arrange a mortgage. Most lenders link the amount they are prepared to borrow to your income and they will want to see evidence that you have a good regular cash flow to support repayments. If you have less than three years' accounts you may find it difficult getting a mortgage at standard rates (*see* page 97).

Your business year

You can choose your own date for the end of your business year. This might be linked to the date you started or it may be the end of the tax or calendar year. Again, seek advice from your accountant as there may be tax advantages to certain dates or you may need to consider seasonal fluctuations in your trade.

You will be taxed on your trading or professional profits for the accounting year that ends in the relevant tax year. So, for example, if you work out your profits to, say, 30 September each year, your 2000–1 calculation will be based on profits for the accounting year that ended on 30 September, 2000. Special rules apply for the year in which you start or end a business.

Self-assessment

Each year in April the Revenue sends out about 8.8m self-assessment forms to taxpayers. Any employee who has been required to complete a return in the past will fall into the self-assessment category, as will anybody whose tax affairs are even remotely complicated (see below).

If you normally pay income tax through the PAYE code or other deduction at source then you probably won't get a return. However, don't think that you are automatically exempt. Under self-assessment, the onus is on you to check whether you need to make a return and, if necessary, to ask for the right forms.

Mean money
The purists will howl at the over-simplification but you can regard national insurance as just another form of taxation.

You need to complete a self assessment return if you are:

- self-employed
- a business partner
- a company director
- an employee or pensioner with 'more complex' affairs
- a trustee or personal representative.

You will also need to complete a form if your tax affairs are 'more complex', for example if you:

- have capital gains of over £7,200 (the exemption limit for 2000–1)
- pay income tax at 40 per cent
- received income from more than one source
- received a lump sum or compensation payment from your employer
- lived abroad for all or part of the tax year in question
- want to claim complicated pension contribution reliefs or tax relief for the more sophisticated investments such as enterprise investment schemes or venture capital trusts.

The basic return has eight pages but you will probably need additional pages or 'schedules'. These cover self-employment, employment and capital gains tax, among other points.

If you are unsure of your position or have any problems with the forms, your local tax office will help. Alternatively you can phone the Inland Revenue's helpline on 0645 000 444 (open weekday evenings from 5 pm to 10 pm, and at weekends from 8 am to 10 pm).

You are required by law to maintain accurate records to support your return. You will need these if the Revenue selects you as a random investigation case or if it suspects you have paid the wrong amount. Keep all documents for at least 22 months after the tax year to which they relate and for five years and ten months if you are self-employed.

31 January is the deadline for filing your tax return for the previous tax year. So, 31 January 2001 will be the deadline for the 1999–2000 tax year.

This is also the time when you have to hand over a big cheque (*see* key dates in Table 6.2). The Revenue tolerates no excuses. It will fine you if you file late and, if your cheque is late, it will charge you on the overdue amount.

Remember that it is vital to get the payments in on time even if you are in dispute with the Revenue about the amount. If you are proved wrong, you will be fined for late payment.

The January tax bill covers two periods. First, there may be an amount outstanding for the previous tax year. The self-employed will already have paid two instalments for that year – in January and July – so the balance may be modest. You may even be entitled to a refund if you overpaid.

Second, you must pay the usual January instalment on account for the next tax year. This is calculated as half of your total bill for the previous tax year.

Morons. I've got morons on my team. Nobody is going to rob us going down the mountain. We have got no money going down the mountain. When we have got the money, on the way back, then you can sweat.

Percy Garris, *Butch Cassidy and the Sundance Kid* (1969)

Mean money
Take a map of the UK and find the furthest point from where you live or work. That is where your tax office will be.

Table 6.2

Remember, the whole system works in advance – so you often end up paying tax for a year before you have actually calculated your correct assessment.

31 January 2001
- Last date for filing your 1999–2000 return. This must include your calculation of tax owed. Penalty for failure: £100 (£200 if it is still outstanding by 31 July 2001).
- Pay outstanding tax for 1999–2000. Penalty for failure: interest is charged on a daily basis from 31 January (currently at 9.5 per cent per annum) on any late payment. In addition 5 per cent surcharge on tax not paid within 28 days; 10 per cent surcharge on tax not paid within 6 months.
- First payment on account for tax year 2001–2. Penalty for failure: interest due from 31 January.

April 2001
Self-assessment tax returns for the 2000–1 tax year issued.

31 July 2001
Pay second instalment of 2000–1 tax. Penalty: interest due from 31 July.

30 September 2001
File your 2000–1 return if you want the Revenue to calculate your tax liability.

5 October 2001
Ask the Revenue for a tax return if you owe tax for the 2000–1 year but have not received a form.

31 January 2002
Final date to file your 2000–1 tax return. Pay outstanding tax for 2000–1. Pay first instalment for 2001–2.

Capital gains tax

The annual exemption of £7,200 for the 2000–1 tax year is the amount of capital gains you can make before you pay capital gains tax (CGT) at your top rate of income tax. CGT is payable when you sell an asset and make a 'chargeable gain' – that is, where the value of the asset has increased since you acquired it.

You only pay tax on the gain – not on the entire value of the asset. Moreover, the government has introduced a desperately complicated way of tapering the amount you should pay depending on how long you have owned the asset. Frankly, unless you are seriously rich, you will not have to pay CGT and if you are *that* rich you can afford a jolly good accountant.

Summary

- If you earn or receive income over the level of the personal allowance in any given tax year (6 April to 5 April) you have to pay income tax.
- Under self-assessment, the onus is on you to check whether you need to make a return and, if necessary, to ask for the right forms.
- When you change jobs your employer will give you a P45 form, which shows your PAYE code, your total earnings and how much tax you have paid since the start of the tax year.
- At the end of each year your employer will give you a P60 form, which shows how much you have earned and how much tax you have paid.

Further information

Try the local tax enquiry centre or tax office. The addresses are in the local telephone book under 'Inland Revenue'.

Most Inland Revenue leaflets are available on the internet at www.open.gov.uk/inrev/irleaf.htm You can also get them from tax offices and tax enquiry centres. Local libraries or the Citizens Advice Bureau (CAB) may also stock them. Useful titles include:

Employed or self-employed? A guide for tax and National Insurance (IR56/NI39)
Income tax and school leavers (IR33)
Income tax and students (IR60)
Tax allowances and reliefs (IR90)
National Insurance contributions for employees (CA01)

Self-assessment (SA/BK8)
Thinking of working for yourself? (IR57)
Starting your own business (CWL1)

Social security benefits

Job seeker's allowance (JSA) is the main benefit for people who are actively seeking work but currently unemployed. The level of benefit will depend partly on how long you have been paying national insurance contributions. You cannot usually get JSA if you are under 18 or if you are studying full time.

The best source of advice on benefits is your local social security office. Ask for leaflet GL19 *School leavers and students*.

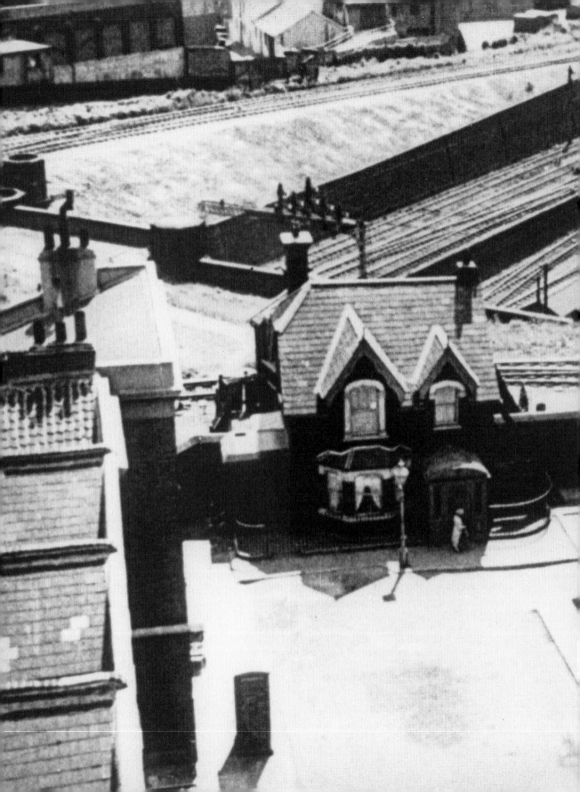

section 3

Room

with **view**

a

But there **must** be a war.

I've paid

a **month's rent** on

the battlefield.

Rufus T Firefly, *Duck Soup* (1933)

[Still from *The Lady Killers*, Canal+Image UK Ltd]

chapter 7

Rising
damp

Your mama's **so**
country she got
in an elevator,
thought it was
a **mobile home**.

Dorothea, *Bebe's Kids* (1992)

After reading this chapter you will:

- hire a private detective to check the landlord is straight before agreeing to rent;

- hire a private detective to check out your best mate or partner before agreeing to share;

- apologize to your mum and stay at home.

Why rent?

If you are under 30 and you are not sure where your next career move will take you, then the more likely question is, 'why buy?'.

Admittedly renting does not give the investment link that property purchase confers, but this whole bricks-and-mortar thing is a bit of a myth unless you stay put for at least five years. Less than this and the costs of buying and selling, combined with the inflexibility of short-term mortgage arrangements, tend to wipe out any gain in the potential rise in property prices.

Renting is a much more immediate solution to accommodation needs. From the financial planning point of view, rent is a known, budgetable cost for a fixed term, which can often be extended.

The rented property market is growing rapidly as more and more people put flexibility before the long-term security of home ownership. In Britain just over 11 per cent of all housing is rented privately and this is rising, although it is nowhere near the 45 per cent figure prevalent in the rest of Europe and in the USA.

Much of the impetus for the growth in the rented private sector came as a result of the Housing Act (1988), which provided a secure and clear legal framework for both tenant and landlord. So, provided you rent through a decent letting agent – preferably one who is a member of the Association of Residential

Letting Agents (ARLA) – your rights and responsibilities will be clear cut.

Association of Residential Letting Agents

ARLA was founded in 1981 as the professional, regulatory and training body for letting agents. If you are going to rent, almost invariably you will need to go to a letting agent and, as the association bluntly puts it:

> Growth markets can attract rank amateurs and even the dishonest. The private rented sector is no exception and ARLA is concerned that the sustained revival in rentals has been shadowed by an increase in the number of unprofessional or cowboy agents.

Members of ARLA have to comply with certain rules, regulations and accounting procedures designed to protect you, the tenant. There are over 1,300 member offices all over the UK, ranging from national chains to small independent specialists and if you want to find one, *see* page 91.

ARLA agents have to have a minimum of two years' experience in the letting and management business before they can join. Among other requirements, they must take out a level of professional indemnity insurance that complies with the association's 'Fidelity Bond', which protects your deposit (*see* below).

Sure, mom, I settle down with a nice girl every night, then I'm free the next morning.

Tommy deVito, *Goodfellas* (1990)

The association is also building up a national database of bad landlords (and tenants!). This will contain the names of landlords reported by members for harassing tenants, withholding the return of deposits without just cause, or failing to comply with safety regulations such as gas checks and servicing.

A fast-moving market

If you are thinking of renting it is unwise to start looking too early. Unlike the property purchase market, rented property can and does move swiftly. The time between first seeing a property you like, making an offer and being ready to move typically is a fortnight. It can be as little as five days.

The renting procedure is explained in detail below, but briefly, when you approach an agent go armed with references to prove you have a regular income. For the employed, a bank or building society reference will probably be enough. The self-employed will need a letter from their accountant or solicitor to verify self-employed earnings. You will also need a reference from your previous landlord, if applicable.

Be prepared to pay the first month's rent up-front and a deposit of four to six weeks' rent, which the agency holds against possible future damages. The deposit should be put in a separate client account.

Despite the speed with which you can sign up and move it is important to have a full inventory and condition report at the outset, so there is no squabbling over who is responsible for the missing teaspoons and the stain on the dining-room carpet when you move out 12 months later.

If you are renting for the first time or have a bad experience behind you, read the ARLA brochure *Trouble-free letting: What every landlord and tenant should ask* (details on page 91). The brochure covers the 24 most important questions about letting. For landlords these include fee structures, inventories, repossessions, legislation, insurance, regulations, and so on. (*See* Chapter 9 on buy-to-let investment opportunities.)

Key considerations

For prospective tenants the most important issues are as follows:

On your own or with friends?

Decide whether you want to live on your own or share. Sharing usually is a lot cheaper both from the point of view of rent per person and bills. The downside is that you have to get on – obviously! Moreover, under the tenancy agreement (*see* below) you are 'jointly and severally responsible' for the property. This means that if your two mates scarper leaving the place trashed and the rent unpaid, you will have to pay the bills. So, if you are going to share, choose your friends wisely.

Mean money
The time between first seeing a property you like, making an offer and being ready to move typically is a fortnight. It can be as little as five days.

> **Mean money**
> It is important to have a full inventory and condition report at the outset so there is no squabbling over who is responsible for the missing teaspoons and the stain on the dining-room carpet when you move out 12 months later.

The agent

The letting agent's role varies but generally he or she will introduce people to a property, prepare the tenancy agreement, advise on inventories, changes to utility accounts and council tax, collect the rent and pay the balance to the landlord's account. If the agent is retained to carry out management services (*see* below) he or she is responsible for paying bills on behalf of the landlord, regularly inspecting the property, and arranging any maintenance work and repairs.

ARLA's Fidelity Bond

The ARLA Bond is a protection of last resort for money entrusted to ARLA members by landlords and tenants during the ordinary course of letting business. If there is a proven theft or fraud by a member agent or its staff and you cannot reclaim your money through the agent or the agent's insurance, you can claim under the Bond. Full details of how this works are available from ARLA.

Should you pay fees to the agent?

ARLA warns flat hunters not to pay an introductory fee but points out that there will be costs to cover – for example inventories and administration, including the preparation of the tenancy agreement and taking up references.

What is a holding deposit?

It is important to remember that paying a holding deposit in no way obliges either party to enter into the tenancy. This is usually a nominal amount that you may be asked to pay when you make an offer to rent a property. If you decide not to proceed by an agreed date this deposit will be retained and used to pay any administrative costs incurred. If you go ahead, it will be offset against the first rent and the full deposit payments. Where it is the landlord who decides not to proceed, you should get the deposit back in full.

The main deposit

Typically, you will be expected to pay a lump sum upfront that includes at least one month's rent in advance and the equivalent of a month to six weeks' rent which will be held as a deposit against damages. The deposit should be placed by the agent in a designated client's account.

What information will the agent need?

The agent will want the addresses of referees who can confirm you are able to pay the rent. These will normally include your bank or building society, employer, your previous landlord if applicable, and, in some cases, your solicitor or accountant.

The tenancy agreement

Your responsibilities should be set out clearly in your tenancy agreement, which you should read carefully before you sign. This is a legally binding document between you and the landlord that applies only to you and to the property you are renting. It should state:

- the rent
- the length of tenancy
- your rights and responsibilities.

Your agreement will most probably be an 'assured' or an 'assured shorthold' tenancy under the Housing Act (1988).

No offence to you, but you are just an assistant. Now, granted, you're my assistant, but still just an assistant. Dawn, on the other hand, is a producer. Her car phone bills are more than your rent.

Buddy Ackerman, *Swimming with Sharks* (1994)

What is 'management'?

It is essential to agree management services at the outset. This is a service provided by the agent to protect and maintain a property to the standard it was at the beginning of the tenancy – fair wear and tear excepted. It includes all maintenance and running repairs, except for any items specifically excluded and any items that are named as the tenant's responsibility in the tenancy agreement.

How long before you can move in?

Normally you should allow about 10 working days for the agent to take up references, clear your cheque covering the first period of rent and the deposit, and arrange for inventories and the transfer of utility accounts into your name. A professional agent will not allow you to move in before all these matters have been settled.

How long is a typical let?

Most agents require the agreement to cover a minimum of six months, but they rarely last longer than one year. Agents will agree the terms for renewal at the outset and include the details in the tenancy agreement.

What if you want to leave early?

If you are likely to leave before the end of

Mean money
If you share and your mates scarper leaving the place trashed and the rent unpaid, you will have to pay the bills.

the term set out in the tenancy agreement it is up to you to negotiate break clauses and have these also written in to the agreement. Without a formal agreement you will be responsible for the rent until the end of the term agreed unless a new tenant can be found who is acceptable to the agent and landlord.

What else do you have to pay for?

As a tenant you are usually responsible for the utility bills – such as gas, water, electricity, and telephone – plus the council tax and the TV licence, among other items.

Mean money
Basically, if it's yours, you need to insure it, so take out contents insurance to replace anything of your own that could be stolen or damaged.

Insurance

Basically, if it's yours, you need to insure it. The landlord is responsible for the buildings insurance and for any contents that are provided such as carpets, furniture, bedding, and kitchen equipment. You will need contents insurance to replace anything of your own that could be stolen or damaged.

If you are at college, the students' union will probably have a cheap insurance deal negotiated with an insurance company. Otherwise speak to an independent insurance broker to get the best rates.

When you move out

Before you leave you must check what you are obliged to do under the tenancy agreement. Usually this means leaving the place clean and tidy, as it was when you moved in. If you leave the place in a mess, a cleaning charge will be deducted from your deposit. Remember to put back any furniture you have moved.

Your deposit

After the landlord or agent has completed an inventory and checked the condition of the flat your deposit should be returned shortly after leaving the property. You cannot set your deposit against the last rent payment.

Summary

- Remember it usually only takes two weeks from seeing a place to moving in, so don't look too soon.

- Use a letting agent who is a member of the Association of Residential Letting Agents (ARLA).

- You will be asked to pay the first month's rent upfront and a deposit of about six weeks' rent.

- If you share, you will be responsible for the bills and rent if your friend lets you down.

- Make sure you have an inventory and condition report done before moving in.

- The tenancy agreement should set out precisely your areas of responsibility and the regular maintenance provided by the agent or landlord.

- If you expect to leave earlier than the standard agreement, or want to be able to renew your tenancy after, say, one year, agree the terms at the outset.

Further information

To get a copy of the ARLA brochure *Trouble-free letting: What every landlord and tenant should ask*, send a stamped addressed envelope to The Association of Residential Letting Agents, Maple House, 53–55 Woodside Road, Amersham, Bucks HP6 6AA. You may also find a copy in your local library and Citizens Advice Bureau. For details of your nearest ARLA member call the ARLA hotline on 01923 896555 Monday to Friday between 9 am and 5.30 pm.

chapter 8

Home
a loan

My collar may be a little frayed, and maybe I need a shoeshine, but nobody's got a mortgage on my soul. I own it. Free and clear.

Lovecraft, *Cast a Deadly Spell* (1991)

After reading this chapter you will:

- practise your 'I can take it or leave it' look in front of the mirror three times a day to avoid showing the estate agents how desperately you want that house;

- employ devious tactics to bring down the tone of the neighbourhood – and hence the prices – in the street where you want to buy;

- start therapy.

Eventually you will probably want to buy your own place. Finding the best way to achieve this can be daunting, not just for the first-time buyer but also to those who have taken a wrong turning and ended up in negative equity trap or with a completely inappropriate mortgage package.

Untangling these complex problems can be an expensive and painful process so it is best to get it right first time around.

There are plenty of sources of advice on mortgages and home ownership but probably the best guide to the basics is published by the Council of Mortgage Lenders (CML) *How to Buy a Home* (*see* page 108). The CML is the central body for the various types of mortgage lender including the banks, building societies, finance houses, insurance companies and specialist mortgage companies. For information on mortgage protection insurance *see* Chapter 16. The Association of British Insurers (ABI) also publishes free fact sheets on mortgage protection and building and contents insurance.

When you decide you want to buy, your first step is to find out what you can afford. Your purchasing power will depend on how much you have already built up in savings and how much you can borrow in the form of a mortgage.

Leasehold *v* freehold

If you buy a property freehold this means you own the land and the bricks and mortar. This is by far the best arrangement. Many properties – particularly flats – are sold on a leasehold basis. This means that you have the right to live in the house or flat for 99 years, or whatever is left on the lease, but once the lease expires the property reverts to the owner.

Leaseholds can prove very troublesome and to a large extent you are at the mercy of the ultimate owner (the freeholder). For example, you are required to maintain the property and pay towards these costs. If the owner lets the property become run down, he or she can demand a considerable sum to do it up and you might not be able to afford this. Some flat owners club together and form a co-operative to buy the freehold to avoid this sort of problem.

If the place you are after is leasehold, do make sure your solicitor checks the terms very carefully indeed.

Seeking advice

How to find the right type of mortgage is the chief subject of this chapter. But first, a word on independent financial advice. Most people can see the sense in approaching an independent financial adviser for a personal pension or any other long-term investment,

yet when it comes to the mortgage the inclination is to think in terms of the lender first. In fact the days when you had to have a building society deposit account for several years and prove your worth as a saver before being granted the privilege of a mortgage are long gone.

These days, provided you have a stable income, there is a huge range of mortgage facilities available and an independent adviser will have access to all the latest offers. He or she will also be able to warn you about the drawbacks of some of the special deals – for example early repayment penalties or lack of flexibility if you want to top up the mortgage at a later date when you move. Given the ease with which advisers can identify the best deal, your time will be better spent considering how you intend to repay the loan.

As with the mortgage itself, the range of repayment options has developed considerably in recent years and some lenders require little more than a verbal assurance that you *will* save one way or another in order to repay the debt. If you opt for an interest-only mortgage backed by an investment plan – for example an individual savings account (Isa) – you are on pure investment ground and will almost certainly benefit from independent advice.

In contrast, most building societies and banks offer a very limited range of options because they are 'tied' to one life office – increasingly their own.

Making an offer

Once you have established the amount you can spend and have found a flat or house you can afford, you can make a formal offer and apply for the loan. The lender will insist on a valuation to check that the property is priced correctly. This is not the same as a structural survey, which is strongly recommended. It is far better to know where the woodworm and dry rot are before you hand over your money.

The mortgage lender will offer you an advance and if the conveyancer, who looks after the legal side of the process, is satisfied that all is

Mean money
There are plenty of people out there who will try one when you are vulnerable and have fallen in love with the home of your dreams. So, watch it and try not to look too enthusiastic.

in order you will proceed to exchange of contract. This is when you make a formal commitment to buy and the owner of the house makes a formal commitment to sell. At this stage usually you will be asked to pay a deposit of up to 10 per cent of the selling price to the conveyancer. A few weeks later, on completion – when you take ownership of the house – you must pay the balance.

Sounds so simple, doesn't it? In practice it's a rough old business and there are plenty of people out there who will try one when you are vulnerable and have fallen in love with the home of your dreams.

I am sick to death of straight people. Tell the truth, aren't you? There's just too goddam many of them. I was in a bank the other day: they were everywhere – writing checks, making deposits. Two of them were applying for a mortgage. It's disgusting. They're taking over.

Buzz Hauser, *Love! Valour! Compassion!* (1997)

So, watch your back and try not to look too enthusiastic.

How much can you borrow?

Lenders differ in the amount they will cough up, but as a rule of thumb expect to be able to borrow up to three times your annual earnings, less any existing commitments such as hire-purchase agreements and other outstanding liabilities. If you want a joint mortgage, the multiple is likely to be three times the higher income plus once the other income, or up to two and a half times the joint income. The lender will want to see confirmation of your income – either a letter from your employer or, if you are self-employed, audited accounts for several previous years. This is when you realize that earning £25,000 but admitting to only £10,000 wasn't such a great idea, even if it did save tax.

Clearly the amount of debt you can comfortably manage will depend on your circumstances. For example, even if you have two decent incomes now it would make sense not to over-commit yourself if you plan to start a family in the near future and expect one of your incomes to reduce substantially or disappear altogether for a few years.

Your mortgage and any capital you set aside from savings towards the house purchase need to cover several items other than the price of the house itself. Surveys, conveyancing fees, stamp duty, land registry fees and the removal costs can all mount up, so ask your adviser or solicitor for a rough idea of the total cost before you put in a formal offer.

Stamp duty is a government tax on the purchase of properties and must be paid where the purchase price exceeds £60,000. The current rate is 1 per cent and this is paid on the full price, not just the tranche that exceeds £60,000. This rises to 4 per cent for purchases between £250,000 and £500,000 and 4 per cent for houses above this level. Land registry fees must also be paid for either registering the title to the property or the transfer where the title has already been registered. The fee for a £100,000–£150,000 house was £230 at the time of writing.

You will also need to consider buildings and contents insurance, life assurance and, depending on existing cover, a payment protection policy.

What is a mortgage?

A mortgage is the legal charge on your property that you give to the lender in return for the loan – a sort of IOU if you like. Together with any special terms and conditions, the mortgage 'deed' is the legal contract between you and the lender. The most important features are:

- the names of the parties to the contract – that is the borrower and the mortgage lender;

- the amount of the loan and your acknowledgement of receipt of the loan;

- a promise by you to repay the loan, with interest, on the stipulated terms – these include the amount of the initial repayments and any special terms, for example a fixed rate or a discount off the lender's variable rate for the first two years;

Mean money

If you breach the terms of your mortgage contract – for example by failing to keep up the monthly payments – the lender has the power to take possession of the property and to sell it in order to recoup the loss.

- the granting of the legal charge of the property to the mortgage lender until the loan is repaid;

- your commitment, if applicable, to any insurance policies and to carry out any repairs and alterations – for example the lender may insist the house is re-roofed within the first three months of ownership to maintain the property's value.

If you breach the terms of your mortgage contract by failing to keep up the monthly payments the lender has the power to take possession of the property and to sell it in order to recoup the loss. Repossessions are a last resort, but unfortunately they were an all too familiar feature of the late 1980s and early 1990s when many borrowers had over-stretched themselves and could not keep pace with the sharp rise in interest rates.

Which type of mortgage?

Repayment

Historically, the most common method was a repayment mortgage where your monthly payments include interest and capital so that at the end of the mortgage term you have paid off the entire debt. This method is regaining its popularity as borrowers tire of the scare stories about endowments.

The interest element in the repayments on the first £30,000 of a loan qualifies for income tax

Table 8.1 Repayments on a £30,000 advance over 25 years at 7 per cent (5.95 per cent after MIRAS)

Year	Annual repayment (£)	Principal (£)	Interest (£)	Balance at year end (£)
1	2,335.66	550.66	1,785.00	29,449.34
2	2,335.66	583.43	1,752.23	28,865.91
3	2,335.66	618.14	1,717.52	28,247.77
4	2,335.66	654.92	1,680.74	27,592.85
5	2,335.66	693.89	1,641.78	26,898.96
6	2,335.66	735.18	1,600.49	26,163.78
7	2,335.66	778.92	1,556.74	25,384.86
8	2,335.66	825.26	1,510.40	24,559.60
9	2,335.66	874.37	1,461.29	23,685.23
10	2,335.66	926.39	1,409.28	22,758.84
11	2,335.66	981.51	1,354.15	21,777.33
12	2,335.66	1,039.91	1,295.75	20,737.41
13	2,335.66	1,101.79	1,233.88	19,635.63
14	2,335.66	1,167.34	1,168.32	18,468.28
15	2,335.66	1,236.80	1,098.86	17,231.48
16	2,335.66	1,310.39	1,025.27	15,921.09
17	2,335.66	1,388.36	947.31	14,532.73
18	2,335.66	1,470.97	864.70	13,061.77
19	2,335.66	1,558.49	777.17	11,503.28
20	2,335.66	1,651.22	684.45	9,852.06
21	2,335.66	1,749.47	586.19	8,102.60
22	2,335.66	1,853.56	482.10	6,249.04
23	2,335.66	1,963.85	371.82	4,285.19
24	2,335.66	2,080.69	254.97	2,204.50
25	2,335.66	2,204.50	131.16	0.00
Total	58,391.57	30,000	28,931	0.00

relief, currently at 15 per cent. The tax relief is taken into account by the lender. So, on the first £30,000, if the mortgage rate is 7 per cent, the tax relief will reduce it to the net rate of 5.95 per cent (85 per cent of 7 per cent). This process is known as mortgage interest relief at source or MIRAS. Under MIRAS you pay the net rate and the borrower reclaims the tax relief from the Inland Revenue.

Most lenders calculate the repayments of a loan up to £30,000 on a constant equal yearly and monthly basis. Table 7.1 shows the constant net repayments on a £30,000 loan advance over 25 years at 7 per cent where the actual repayments are 5.95 per cent after MIRAS.

Some lenders may calculate the monthly payments on an 'increasing net' basis. Under this system the lender calculates the tax relief due on the interest you pay in a given year and deducts this sum from your gross repayments. This means the mortgage repayments are made net of tax relief and you will obtain the maximum tax relief in the first years of the mortgage. However, because the amount of interest you pay decreases as you repay the capital, the amount of tax relief you receive also decreases, so your monthly repayments will increase over time.

Clearly, if you have a mortgage on a standard variable rate – or a discount of this – your repayments will rise and fall in line with the corresponding fluctuations in the lender's variable rate, which in turn is affected by interest rates set by the Bank of England.

To simplify administration, lenders often calculate the interest payments at the start of its financial year for the whole of that year, so this will not take account of any extra capital repayments you make.

Interest only

The alternative to a repayment mortgage is an interest-only loan where you make interest payments each month but the capital debt remains static. At the same time you save through an investment vehicle and at the end of the mortgage term you aim to build up a large enough fund to repay the mortgage and, possibly, create a surplus lump sum for your own use. Unless you go for an endowment (not a good idea) you also need to take out sufficient life assurance to repay the loan if you or your partner dies before your fund has grown to the required level.

For details on how Isas and other suitable investments work, see Section 4.

Your choice of interest rates

These days it is very rare for a new borrower not to be able to find some sort of special deal on the interest rate. Your financial adviser will be able to run through the complete range at the time you wish to take out the loan, but this section describes briefly your main options. Bear in mind, as always, that there is no such thing as a free lunch. Somewhere along the line you must pay for the special feature, which usually means committing yourself to a minimum number of years with that lender or facing a penalty if you want to switch to a different mortgage or repay a capital lump sum to reduce the outstanding debt.

Annual percentage rate

Before looking at the various options it is helpful to understand how the interest rate is calculated and applied. There are many variations on this theme – for example a lender might calculate and charge the interest on a daily, monthly, quarterly or even annual basis, all of which affect the annual rate charged.

To enable you to make meaningful comparisons between lenders' offers, the government introduced the concept of the 'annual percentage rate of change' or APR. This represents the total charge for credit and takes into account the added costs of the loan, such as the valuation fees and lender's conveyancing charges, which are not included in the nominal rate. The APR is based on the gross rate of interest so it does not take account of MIRAS.

One word of warning. The APR quoted for fixed rate or discount schemes only applies to the offer period – it does not take into

account the full variable rate which will kick in after the cheap rate has finished.

Variable rate

Lenders frequently change the interest rates and these increases and decreases are passed on to your monthly repayments. Where the institution has borrowers and savers – the building societies and banks for example – they need to retain a margin between the two as this represents their 'turn'. If they have to pay more to savers to keep rates competitive they will have to pass on this increase to mortgage customers. Other factors that influence mortgage rates include fluctuations in the Bank of England's base rate and, for the 'centralized' lenders, the cost of raising funds on the money markets.

Fixed rate

This type of mortgage is particularly attractive to borrowers who want the comfort of knowing what their liabilities are for several years in order to budget accurately. Typically, lenders are prepared to fix the rate for one or two years, sometimes up to five. When the fixed-rate period ends you would switch to the lender's variable rate or you might be offered the chance to fix again.

The factors that influence a decision to go for a fixed rate as a borrower are similar to the considerations facing a saver – but in reverse.

If general interest rates rise you will be protected from an increase in your repayments for the period covered. However, if interest rates fall you will be locked into an uncompetitively high rate.

Just as with savers who go for a fixed-rate bond, fixed rate borrowers must watch out for early redemption penalties. Quite often these are so high that you are forced to stay put because it is too expensive to get out, even when you take into account much better rates elsewhere.

Discounted rates

Most lenders offer a discount of 1 per cent or 2 per cent off their variable rate, usually for a period of one or two years. On top of this a lender may provide a 'cashback' where a lump sum is paid to the borrower once the mortgage has been settled. This type of package can be very attractive if you want to keep payments down during the first few years, but if you are interested do make sure you fully understand the penalties for early redemption or for repaying part of your debt with a lump sum. In the latter case you would forfeit the cashback and you would have to pay, typically, the difference between the discount and standard variable rate on the lump sum you use to reduce the mortgage.

Under this system the longer you stick with

the lender, the worse the partial repayment penalty will be – until, that is, you are clear of the penalty period.

Cap-and-collar mortgages

Under a cap-and-collar mortgage the lender sets an upper and lower limit on fluctuations in the interest rate. This means you know the worst in advance – the rate cannot exceed the upper limit. However, if interest rates fall below the 'collar', you will be stuck with an uncompetitive package, just as you would be with a fixed-rate mortgage. Penalties are likely to apply if you want to remortgage to take advantage of better rates elsewhere.

Mortgage-related insurance

Due to the substantial size of the loan and the value of the property, it is important to make sure you have the right type of insurance. In some cases this will be a compulsory requirement by the lender, although usually you can choose your own insurer so, as ever, do shop around or use an independent financial adviser to do so for you. It may seem easier at the time to go with the lender's choice but this may prove an expensive mistake.

Buildings and contents insurance are essential and both the CML and ABI guides (*see* page 108) offer some good advice for buyers. In this chapter, however, we limit the examination to the mortgage-related insurance that protects the lender if you default, and the personal insurances that either pay off the debt in the event of your death or help you maintain repayments in the event of long-term illness.

Mortgage indemnity

Financial institutions like to protect themselves if they lend you more than 75 per cent of the value of the property. The risk they face is that if you default they would need to repossess the house and sell it, probably for less than the purchase price given they wouldn't want to keep an empty property on their books in order to wait for prices to rise. So, if you want a 'high loan to value' advance, lenders reckon they are justified in making you pay towards the mortgage indemnity insurance, which would reimburse them for some or all of the difference between the outstanding mortgage and the actual selling price.

The important point to remember about the mortgage indemnity fee (it might also be called an additional security fee or high percentage loan fee) is that it protects the lender, not you.

Life assurance

Life assurance is examined in Chapter 16 but briefly, your life assurance should pay off all your outstanding liabilities. The mortgage is likely to be your main debt but you should also factor in any other liabilities whether they are debts or regular commitments.

There are several types of life assurance, but the simplest and cheapest is likely to be level-term assurance, which provides a lump sum if you die during the insured period but nothing if you do not. If you have dependants – particularly a non-working partner and children – your life assurance should provide a lump sum which, when invested, would generate a replacement income, taking into account any company benefits such as dependants' pensions and lump-sum death benefits. You should also consider family income benefit or some other type of life assurance to cover the partner who looks after the children. Family income benefit could, for example, be used to pay for a live-in nanny to enable the surviving spouse to continue to work.

Payment protection

This is a variation on critical illness and/or permanent health insurance (PHI – *see* Chapter 16). If you suffer a chronic illness or become disabled, this type of policy would cover the cost of the mortgage and any related costs – insurances for example. The critical illness element would provide a lump sum if you suffered a major illness.

You might also be offered a third type of policy, known as accident, sickness and unemployment (ASU) insurance. This covers your monthly mortgage payments if you become too ill to work or are unemployed.

The accident and sickness element is like a short-term PHI policy. Unemployment insurance is available through a few specialist insurers but generally is very expensive, so ASU may be the only way to get it. Following social security changes, if you are a new borrower you now have to wait nine months before you can claim unemployment benefit to cover your mortgage – longer if you have savings of £8,000 or more. You can use ASU to insure the nine-month gap and in some cases can cover yourself for up to two years.

However, experts warn you should treat this type of insurance as a way of buying some breathing space if you need to reassess your finances in the light of illness or unemployment. It does not provide a long-term replacement income.

The same caveat applies to the limited versions of PHI and critical illness offered through a mortgage protection scheme. The main point to note here is that, while the lender is concerned to ensure you keep up your monthly repayments, in practice you will need a great deal more than this to cover all your monthly outgoings and your liabilities. This is particularly important if you are self-employed and therefore not covered by an employer's group scheme at work.

Read the small print

Simplified acceptance for life assurance

This is a shortcut to buying the life assurance you need to cover your mortgage debt if you die. Buying life assurance can be time consuming and often involves completing a detailed questionnaire and attending a private medical. However, some providers will insure you without these requirements if you are under age 50 and need less than £70,000 of cover. To qualify, usually you must also provide satisfactory responses to three questions about whether you have visited your GP in the last few months, whether you are taking medication and whether you have had an HIV test, counselling or advice. You might also be asked if you have any dangerous pastimes – motor racing or hang gliding for example.

Free temporary life cover

Once you exchange contracts you are legally bound to the mortgage but your life cover may not take effect until completion. To avoid the potential complications that would arise if a borrower died in the period between exchange and completion, some companies provide free cover for up to three months from exchange.

Transfers from joint to single life

Given that one marriage in three ends in divorce, it is important to check your policy will not need to be cancelled if the ownership of the house and endowment have to change from joint to single ownership. This is particularly important where your life assurance and investment are combined through an endowment, since policies stopped in the early years are usually very poor value. Rather than cancel the policy on divorce, some providers allow one of the partners to continue the premiums unchanged, or they might alter the life assurance and premiums to reflect the new ownership.

Guaranteed insurability options

This gives you the flexibility to increase the level of life assurance if you move house, improve your home or if your family situation changes, for example on marriage or on the birth of a child. Some insurers will increase cover without a medical examination or detailed application form.

Mortgage-related investments

Endowments

The main difference between endowments and other investments is that endowments combine life assurance with the savings plan. Where you use other investments to back a mortgage – an individual savings account for example – you have to buy life assurance separately.

One of the big selling features of endowments in the 1970s and early 1980s was life assurance premium relief (LAPR). This was abolished for new endowments taken out after March 1984.

In recent years endowments have faced serious criticism. Evidence of widespread 'churning' for extra sales commission in the mid- to late 1980s, when investors were persuaded to cancel an existing policy and take out a new product, tarnished the endowment's reputation. Many policyholders also assumed that the endowment guaranteed to pay off the mortgage at maturity. In fact this was never guaranteed, but it has taken a period of falling returns to bring this point home.

As with any investment, the size of the fund at maturity depends largely on three factors:

- the amount you pay to the financial institution;
- the amount actually invested after charges and the cost of the life assurance are deducted;
- the investment performance.

We gonna **be quittin'** all this, **as soon** as the **hard** times are over. I can tell **ya that**. **Why** just the other night, me and Bonnie **were talkin'**. And we **were talkin'** about **the time** we're **gonna settle down** and get us **a home**.

Clyde Barrow, *Bonnie and Clyde* (1967)

As a general rule, therefore, you would be better off with an individual savings account and taking out the necessary life assurance separately.

Individual savings accounts

In Chapter 11 we explain why in most cases unit-trust and investment-trust-based Isas are more tax efficient than endowments, since the funds grow free of income and capital gains tax and there is no further tax liability on withdrawals. You can also pay what you want, when you want, provided you stick to the overall Revenue annual limits.

Isa mortgages are similar to unit-linked endowment mortgages. However, instead of using an endowment plan to cover both the life assurance and savings required to pay off the debt, with an Isa mortgage the Isa is used as the savings vehicle and a separate life assurance policy is taken out to pay off the debt in the event of the death of one of the borrowers.

Mean money
Individual savings accounts are more tax efficient and more flexible than endowments.

In response to criticism, several leading endowment companies have altered their product structure to offer better value and greater flexibility – in particular by improving their terms for investors who stop a policy early. However, there are still some pretty awful endowments around that combine poor performance, high charges and are so inflexible that once you are in it is very hard to get out again without losing a lot of money.

Isas *v* endowments: tax and charges

To summarize, there are two important differences between endowments and Isas that affect the return, namely tax and charges.

The Isa fund grows free of tax while the endowment fund suffers a tax on income at a rate broadly equivalent to the basic rate of tax. Understandably, tax efficiency is the main feature promoted by Isa companies.

Isas also score in terms of the timing and distribution of charges, which usually are spread evenly throughout the investment period. With endowments, often a large proportion of the sales, marketing and administration charges that relate to the whole investment period are deducted during the first year or two, so if you stop the plan in the early years you may get next to nothing back.

Advisers warn that in most cases it is unwise to stop endowment payments due to the impact of those high early charges. However, you could use an Isa to top up the mortgage if there is a need to increase the loan.

Pension mortgages

The tax-free cash available at retirement from pension arrangements can be used to repay a mortgage. As is explained in Chapter 15, with a pension plan you get full tax relief on premiums and the fund itself grows free of tax. The pension itself is taxed as income.

In theory then, a personal pension plan should make a very tax-efficient repayment vehicle – but there is an important caveat. If you fund your mortgage solely from this source you could leave yourself short in retirement.

Summary

- Seek independent financial advice on both the choice of mortgage and on the investment plan you use to repay the debt.

- Most mortgage institutions will lend up to three times your annual salary, two and a half times your joint salary, or three times the main and once the second salary.

- Do check the penalties that apply to any special offers such as a fixed rate or discount on the variable rate.

- Use the annual percentage rate (APR) to make comparisons between different lenders, but remember this will only relate to the offer period if there is a discount or fixed rate.

- Make sure your life assurance and income protection plans cover all your liabilities and requirements, not just what you need to repay the mortgage.

- Isas are more tax efficient and flexible than endowments.

- Pension mortgages are very tax efficient, but be careful not to deplete your fund to the point where you end up with a low income in retirement.

Further information

Council of Mortgage Lenders: for a free guide *How to Buy a Home* or *How to Buy a Home in Scotland*, send a large stamped addressed envelope to the Council of Mortgage Lenders, BSA/CML Bookshop, 3 Savile Row, London W1X 1AF. The CML also publishes a free leaflet on taxation and the homebuyer.

Association of British Insurers: for free fact sheets on mortgage protection insurance, buildings and contents insurance, write to the Association of British Insurers, 51 Gresham Street, London EC2V 7HQ.

chapter 9

The caretaker

Well, bye Pete. Later, Pete. Listen, don't forget to write, Pete. And remember, the door's always open to ya, Pete. You can come home to the pad and all your friends. But write first 'cos we're renting your room!

Micky, *The Monkees* (1966)

After reading this chapter you will:

- see people as a source of income;

- move your granny into a nursing home and rent out her house;

- give up socialism altogether.

Business opportunities in property

Some 2 million households rent through the private sector in the UK. According to the letting agents there is a national shortage of rental property in every area from the executive home to the studio flat.

An increasing number of people decide to keep their first house or flat when they move on. If you think it is a desirable property for short-term lets you may well be able to cover your mortgage and other costs, *and* make a profit. This has proved particularly true of property in the South East where the demand for rented accommodation is high.

The alternative is to go and buy somewhere with the sole intention of renting it out. If you have capital to invest and are comfortable with the idea of taking out another mortgage, then you might do well out of a buy-to-let scheme. The average gross return on rental income in Britain today is about 8–10 per cent. The gross return is the amount you receive before deducting the costs of letting (including the mortgage where applicable) and the management fees. Capital appreciation is likely to match, if not exceed, retail-price inflation for the foreseeable future.

Bear in mind though these figures assume the property is let continuously. If you do not choose your property with care it may stand empty for several months at a time, which will put a serious dent in your return.

And as for this non-college bullshit, I got two words for that: learn to f*****' type, 'cause if you're expecting me to help out with the rent you're in for a big f*****' surprise.

Mr Pink, *Reservoir Dogs* (1992)

Financial health warning!

If you buy residential property directly, rather than through a pooled fund such as an authorized unit trust, you are not covered by the Financial Services Act, even if you purchase through an independent adviser who is regulated by the Financial Services Authority. This means that you have no protection if you are given bad advice or if the properties in which you invest turn out to be poor quality. *Caveat emptor*!

Taxation

Taxation is discussed in Chapter 6. As far as investment property is concerned, net rental income (that is after expenses) is subject to income tax at your marginal rate

Mean money
If you buy residential property directly, rather than through a pooled fund such as an authorized unit trust, you are not protected by the Financial Services Act.

Mean money
An increasing number of people decide to keep their first house or flat when they move on and rent it out.

(22 per cent or 40 per cent in 2000–1). Expenses include the loan interest. Furthermore, a wear and tear allowance of 10 per cent of the rent, less water rates, is available where the property is furnished.

Any growth in the value of the property between purchase and sale is subject to capital gains tax (CGT) although the actual amount will depend on the length of time you have held the property as an investment.

Buy to let

'Buy to let' is the initiative launched by the
Association of Residential Letting Agents
(ARLA – see page 91) and is supported by
eight major mortgage lenders: Alliance &
Leicester, Capital Home Loans, Clydesdale
Bank, First Active, Halifax Mortgage Services,
Mortgage Express, NatWest Mortgage Services
and Paragon Mortgages.

Its aim is to stimulate the rented property
market by encouraging private investors to
take advantage of low interest rates and the
medium to long-term potential for capital
growth in property.

The loan

Historically, investors in property who wanted
to raise a loan found that lenders imposed a
hefty surcharge on retail mortgage rates and
would not take the rental income into
consideration when calculating the maximum
loan. Now many lenders – including those in
the buy-to-let scheme – offer rates
comparable to those extended to owner-
occupiers and take the rental income into
account when assessing the maximum loan
that you can service.

Loans can be arranged for a single property or
a mini-property investment portfolio of up to
five houses and flats. Loans of between
£15,000 and £1 million per investor are
available for periods of between five and 45

years. Typically, the loan will cover up to 80
per cent of the valuation.

Methods of servicing the loan are flexible in
most cases and mirror terms available to
owner-occupiers (see Chapter 8). There are
even loans that allow for overpayment and use
the surplus to provide a repayment holiday or
to cover future periods when you may be
short of cash if the property is temporarily
empty.

Which type of property?

ARLA's advice is to keep your choice of buy-to-
let property simple: 'The common
denominators sought by potential tenants are
location, amenities and facilities.' Don't make
the mistake of buying somewhere quaint
because you could see *yourself* being very
happy there. 'Ignore personal tastes and avoid
property with potential maintenance problems
such as a lot of woodwork or a large garden.
These features will add nothing to the rental
value but cost a lot to keep up,' ARLA warns.

Before you buy it is wise to seek the advice of
a letting agent who will be able to give you
the low-down on whether it will rent out
easily. You need to find out about local
demand – whether it's for four-bedroomed
houses or flats, how many bathrooms are
required per number of bedrooms, and
whether gardens and patios add to rental
value or just to your maintenance costs.

Mortgage lenders may have their own stipulations. For example they may not like properties with more than one kitchen and four or five bedrooms in case they are converted to bedsits.

Transport is a key issue. In some areas you can expect tenants to be commuters and so you need to consider how far away is the nearest bus route, railway station or tube station.
Alternatively, can people park outside the flat or house?

This is **my** beat, **my** house, **I carry** a mortgage. Someone has been refilling the **toilet paper dispenser** in the bathroom **so** that the **toilet paper** comes out *under* the roll . . . **I hate that!**

Dad, *Roundhouse* (1992)

> **Mean money**
> If you do not choose your property with care it may stand empty for several months at a time, which will put a serious dent in your return.

The letting agent

About 50 per cent of rentals are arranged through letting and managing agents, most – but not all – of which are members of recognized professional organizations.

We considered the role of the letting agent from the point of view of the tenant in Chapter 7. If you are a landlord the agent will act as your guard dog, helping to protect an expensive asset by selecting reliable tenants and looking after the property in your absence. A good agent will vet tenants carefully and make sure there is the minimum amount of time between lets.

In return the agent will deduct a percentage of the rent for his or her services. This will vary depending on the size and type of property and whether you want the agent to look after the maintenance as well. Typically, you could expect an ARLA agent to charge 10 per cent of the rent for finding the tenant and to cover the inventory and paperwork. If you want a full management agreement, where the agent stands *in loco parentis*, as it were, you can expect to pay an additional 5–7 per cent. Remember, these fees are tax deductible.

After a tenant's offer has been accepted the agent is responsible for taking up references and making credit checks before preparing to change the utility accounts and drawing up the tenancy agreement (*see* page 88). The agent will also need to make an inventory of all the furnishings and fittings and will write up a condition report so that any damages can be assessed and a suitable deduction made from the tenant's deposit where necessary. Both the tenant and landlord should be present when these are compiled and should sign each other's copies.

Rentals tend to be short term – typically six months to three years. Most lets, unless for very high rentals, are arranged under an assured shorthold tenancy. This covers tenancies from six months upwards but usually there would be a cap at 12 months with an option to renew. This will list all the do's and don'ts and set out any rules, for example on children and pets.

Summary

Do:

- Think of buying to let as a medium to long-term investment.

- Seek advice from an ARLA letting agent on local market demand.

- Get your sums right. Will the rent cover borrowings and costs after allowing for void periods (when the property is empty)?

- Decorate to a high standard and fit out kitchens and bathrooms well to attract the best tenants and to keep the property let out.

- Use an ARLA agent or someone who can offer a similar level of protection (*see* page 85).

Don't:

- Let personal taste cloud your judgement when choosing a property to buy to let.

- Purchase anywhere that needs a high level of maintenance.

- Think of leaving the running of an investment property to friends and relatives in your absence. Tenants require a full management service.

- Use off-the-shelf tenancy agreements from HMSO or law stationers.

- Forget to issue the right notices or to have a proper inventory and condition report drawn up before the tenant moves in.

- Furnish with second-hand furniture or cast-off soft furnishings. This will probably contravene the fire and furnishing regulations.

Further information

The ARLA hotline is open from Monday to Friday 9 am to 5.30 pm. Telephone 01923 896555 for details of the nearest ARLA agent, the mortgage lenders on the buy-to-let panel and the recognized buy-to-let mortgage brokers for your region.

A **fistful** of **dollars**

Investors would do **well** to remember Loacon's law of improbable generosity: '**Don't** look a **gift** horse in the mouth, but do **check** for Greek soldiers elsewhere in **its** anatomy'.

Michael Becket,
Bluff Your Way in Finance
Ravetta Books (1995)

[Still from *The Lady Killers*, Canal+Image UK Ltd]

chapter 10

The
money
pit

Finance **is** a **gun**. Politics **is** knowing **when** to **pull** the **trigger.**

Don Lucchese,
The Godfather Part III (1990)

After reading this chapter you will:

- understand investment risk and be afraid – very afraid;

- still not understand derivatives;

- throw away that dodgy jacket that makes you look like a futures trader.

When it comes to investment there's no such thing as too cynical. The markets are run by sinners wearing Gucci, not saints wearing sackcloth. You need these people though, so it helps if you understand a bit about what they do and why. Money is inherently lazy. It doesn't grow on trees and it doesn't grow at all unless you nurture it or steal it.

Unfortunately, savings and investment institutions are adept at dressing up what are essentially quite straightforward assets. As a result, it is easy to fall into the trap of investing in 'Isas' or 'pensions' without being aware of the underlying investments and how they fit in with your other savings. If you have more than one Isa or pension, plus a few shares in your company and the building society that demutualized, you've probably got the investment equivalent of a dog's dinner.

This chapter explains the characteristics of the asset classes you will come across in your quest for the best investments. Among other things it will give you confidence to challenge advisers who try to blind you with science and baffle you with jargon. Go ahead and call their bluff.

Risk

Crucial to your understanding of investments is your attitude to risk. The technical definition of risk, in financial terms, is 'the standard deviation of the (arithmetic) average return'. It might be fun to discuss this at a dinner party but only if you don't want to be invited back.

For most people the meaning of risk can be expressed more simply. The biggest perceived risk is the loss of your original capital. Equally important, however, is the loss of the real value of your capital through inflation. Now, there is no such thing as a 'safe' investment or saving scheme, but some are safer than others in terms of protecting your original capital. On the other hand, they may not protect you from inflation.

Before looking at what different types of investment set out to achieve, it is helpful to look at the underlying asset classes in which you will invest.

Securities

Investment literature deliberately uses a lot of confusing jargon. Commonly used (and misused) terms include 'securities', 'stocks' and 'shares'.

'Securities' is the general name for all stocks and shares. What we call 'shares' today, originally were known as 'stocks' because they represented part ownership in the joint stock companies – the precursors to today's public limited companies (or plcs). So, to some extent the terms stocks and shares are interchangeable, and we still use the terms *stock*markets and *stock*brokers.

Broadly speaking, stocks are fixed-interest securities and shares are the rest. The four main types of securities listed and traded on the UK Stock Exchange are:

- *UK equities*: ordinary shares issued by over 2,000 UK companies – use the term

It's **not** a question of **enough**, pal. It's a **zero sum game**, somebody **wins**, somebody **loses**. Money itself **isn't** lost or made, it's **simply** transferred from **one** perception **to another**.

Gekko, *Wall Street* (1987)

'domestic' equities and you will look cool;

- *Overseas equities*: ordinary shares issued by non-UK companies;

- *Bonds*: fixed-interest stocks issued by companies and local authorities, among others – think of them as a sophisticated type of IOU;

- *Gilts*: bonds issued by the UK government to raise money to fund any shortfall in public expenditure.

If a company wants to raise finance it has two main options. It can sell part of the ownership of the company by issuing ordinary shares (equities) or it can borrow money by issuing bonds. All you need to create a market is organizations with something to sell and organizations that want to buy. Shares and bonds are bought and sold on the stockmarket.

UK equities

Equities are the quoted shares of companies in the UK and tend to dominate most portfolios, whether they are held directly or are pooled through collective funds such as unit trusts, open-ended investment companies, investment trusts or insurance funds.

The return achieved by UK equities, when measured over the long term, has exceeded both price and earnings inflation. Your aim – or the aim of your investment manager – is to invest in companies that will achieve a good return for your money in exchange for an acceptable level of risk.

A share or equity literally entitles the owner to a specified share in the profits of the company and, if the company is wound up, to a specified share of its assets.

The owner of shares is entitled to the dividends – the six-monthly distribution to shareholders of part of the company's profits. The 'dividend yield' on equities is the dividend paid by a company divided by that company's share price.

There is no set redemption date for an equity when the company is obliged to return your original investment. If, as a shareholder, you want to convert your investment into cash ('to realize its value') you must sell your shares.

Share classes

To add to the fun, there are different classes of shares. Most investors buy ordinary shares, which give the holder the right to vote on the constitution of the company's board of directors. Since this is the most common type of share, the term 'ordinary' usually is dropped, unless it is to distinguish the shares from a different category.

Preference shares carry no voting rights but have a fixed dividend payment, so can be attractive to those seeking a regular income. These shares have 'preference' over ordinary shareholders if the company is wound up – hence the name.

Equity-related investments

There are several sub-classes of equities or equity-related investments.

Convertibles and warrants

Convertibles and warrants are special types of shares that have characteristics that make them attractive in certain circumstances.

Convertibles are more akin to bonds (see below), in that they pay a regular income and have a fixed redemption date. However, a convertible confers the right to convert to an ordinary share or preference share at a future date. This can be an attractive proposition if the price is attractive on the convertible date.

Warrants confer a right but not an obligation on the holder to convert to a specific share at a predetermined price and date. The value of the warrant, which itself is traded on the stockmarket, is determined by the difference or premium of the share price over the conversion price of the warrant.

Derivatives

Derivatives, as the name suggests, derive their value from the price of an underlying security. This is the generic term given to futures contracts and options, both of which can be used to reduce risk in an institutional fund or, in the case of options, even in a large private portfolio.

A futures contract binds two parties to a sale or purchase at a specified future date. The price is fixed at the time the contract is taken out. These futures contracts can be used by institutional funds to control risk because they allow the manager to quickly increase or reduce the fund's exposure to an existing asset class. Futures have also proved popular as a cost-cutting mechanism, particularly in index-tracking funds and other funds where there are rapid changes of large asset allocations.

Options allow you, for a down payment, to have the right but not the obligation to buy or sell something at an agreed price on a specific date. Some private investors use options as a type of insurance policy to protect their portfolio against a fall in the market.

Overseas equities

These are similar in principle to UK equities but there are differences in shareholder rights.

Investment overseas provides exposure to the growth in foreign markets, including younger, fast growing economies. However, these shares also expose you to different economic and political risks, as well as to currency fluctuations. This can be both good and bad, of course, but the point is that it adds an extra layer of risk.

As a rule of thumb, exposure to the major developed economies, for example the European Union countries, the US, and Canada, is considered beneficial but generally is achieved through collective funds – for example investment trusts (*see* page 140). Exposure to the emerging economies is high risk and so only suitable for those prepared to take a punt.

Bonds

UK bonds are issued by borrowers. Where the borrower is the government these bonds are known as gilt-edged securities, or just 'gilts'. Where the borrower is a company, the instruments are known as bonds or, more accurately, 'corporate bonds'. Bonds are also issued by local authorities, overseas governments and overseas companies.

In return for the loan of your money, the borrower agrees to pay a fixed rate of interest (known as the coupon) for the agreed period and to repay your original capital sum on a specified date, known as the maturity or redemption date.

The point to remember about fixed-interest securities is that the investment return is determined more by the level of interest rates than the issuing company's profitability. Assuming the issuer remains sufficiently secure to honour the future coupon payments (the regular interest) and redemption payment (the return of the original capital), you know exactly what your return will be, *provided* you hold the bond to maturity. Gilts offer the highest degree of security because they are issued by the UK government.

Trading bonds

If you or a fund manager sell a bond before its maturity date, then the value of the future coupon and redemption payments will depend on the prevailing interest rates at the time of sale.

So, if interest rates are rising, then the value of the fixed-interest security will fall. This is because, for the same amount of capital invested, you could get a better return elsewhere. Conversely, if interest rates are falling, then the value of the fixed-interest security will be higher, because it provides a greater stream of income than you could get from alternative sources.

This volatile pattern of behaviour is more apparent with fixed-interest securities that have a long period to run to maturity, since they are more likely to be traded before redemption date.

To summarize, as a general rule equities are considered more risky and volatile than bonds because they behave in an unpredictable way whereas, provided the company or government backing a bond is watertight, the return on a bond *held to maturity* is predictable. However, it is not predictable if you decide to sell before maturity.

Index-linked gilts

Index-linked gilts are issued by the UK government and are guaranteed to provide interest payments (the coupon) and a redemption value, which increase in line with annual inflation. For this reason they are one of the lowest risk assets for income seekers, although they may not necessarily provide a competitive return.

Cash

'Cash' does not mean stacks of £20 notes stuffed under the mattress but usually refers to money on deposit. Deposits have the advantage that the value in monetary terms is known and is certain at all times. What is unknown is the interest that will be received and by how much this may fall short of the rate of inflation.

Property

In investment terms, 'property' usually refers to the ownership of land and buildings that are used by a business or other organization. The owner of the property receives income from the rent charged to the tenant and, over time, this rent is expected broadly to keep pace with inflation. The dominant factor in the value of a property is the desirability or otherwise of its location.

Mean money

As a general rule equities are considered more risky and volatile than bonds because they behave in an unpredictable way whereas, provided the company or government backing a bond is watertight, the return on a bond *held to maturity* is predictable.

There are several problems with property. First, it is often sold in large blocks that cannot be easily split for investment purposes. As a result, only the larger institutional funds can afford (or are wise) to own property directly. Second, property is a very illiquid asset and it can take several years for the right selling conditions to arise.

Risk and reward

When you take a risk – for example by investing in equities rather than putting your money on deposit – you expect a commensurate reward.

The reward for investors is the total return, which is usually expressed as a percentage increase of the original investment. This may be a combination of income (or yield) plus capital growth (or rise in the market price).

Risk is very subjective. Like beauty, it is in the eye of the beholder. To help you gauge your attitude to risk it is helpful to consider the twin evils mentioned above – inflation risk and capital risk.

Inflation risk

Savings and investments that expose you to inflation risk usually fall into the 'safe' category. For example, we all tend to think of bank and building society deposit accounts as risk free. But are they? If you are worried

about the risk of losing your original capital then, provided you stick to the well-regulated UK building societies and banks, you can put your money on deposit and your original capital will be safe.

Your capital will not diminish, indeed it will grow, assuming income is reinvested. However, the growth will be modest and in real (that is, inflation-adjusted) terms, it may not always match the rate of inflation.

This does not mean you should ignore deposit accounts. In practice they play a very important part in financial planning for the short and medium term.

Capital risk

Historically, if you wanted to match or beat inflation over the long term you would have had to invest in equities, although in recent years the gap between bonds and equities has narrowed. With equities, unless your fund offers a guarantee (and these can be costly – see page 139), your capital certainly is at risk. So, when you see the statutory wealth warning that your investment can go down as well as up, take it seriously.

The importance of spreading risk

Risk can be managed in different ways. You can concentrate it in a single investment or spread it over a wide range. For example, if you invest all your money in the shares of just

After 'When should I buy my holiday money?' the next most commonly asked question is 'What are derivatives?' The best answer to give is, 'They are highly geared financial instruments that enable investors to both hedge and speculate at relatively little outlay.' It is usually advisable to move the conversation rapidly to something a little easier, like the theory of relativity.

Stuart Trow, *Bluffers' Guide to Economics,* Ravetta Publishing (1996)

one company and it does well you will be in clover. If the company goes bust you could lose the lot.

It is wise to spread risk by investing in a range of shares, either directly or through collective funds such as unit and investment trusts.

Note, however, that even with collective funds the risk rating varies considerably. At one end of the spectrum are the higher risk specialist funds that tend to be small and managed on an aggressive basis. At the other, more comfortable end, are the large UK equity

Mean money
When you see the statutory wealth warning that your investment can go down as well as up, take it seriously.

or international funds that offer greater immunity to the capricious behaviour of stockmarkets. Bear in mind, though, that even the most broadly diversified funds will be hit when stockmarkets crash.

You can protect yourself further from risk if you diversify into different asset classes – for example, instead of just investing in UK equities, you could include some overseas equities, bonds, gilts, deposits and, possibly, property in your portfolio. Each asset class behaves in a different way and therefore a careful asset allocation will protect you from swings in the economic cycle. Institutional pension funds, for example, invest across all the main asset classes, although the biggest proportion is in UK equities.

Inflation and your returns

It is also important to keep in mind the relationship between inflation and returns. At the time of writing the government's aim was to keep inflation under 2.5 per cent. This is based on a definition of retail price inflation that excludes mortgage interest payments.

Inflation is a key determinant of the real investment return. Stockmarkets may not be prepared for a sudden rise or fall in inflation but they tend to adjust over time and provide a long-term hedge against price rises. Gilts and cash are not considered suitable as a long-term hedge against inflation.

Period of investment

Clearly, long-term past returns on equities, gilts and cash should be viewed with some caution and certainly should not be treated as a guide to the future. While history indicates that equities should provide a better return than bonds over the *medium to long term*, there is an important caveat.

'Medium' term means a minimum of five years. Long term is more like 10–15 years. If you go into the stockmarkets for shorter periods you are in danger of getting your fingers burned either because the markets take a tumble just before you want to get out or because the fixed costs associated with buying your investments undermine the return in the early years.

The importance of scale

It is rarely wise for a private investor to imitate the style of an institutional fund manager, but it is interesting to watch how they behave. The large pension funds, for example, are worth millions of pounds. Some run into billions. This means they can make money on minor price changes due to the sheer volume of their transactions. Moreover, compared with an individual investor, institutional funds benefit from very low dealing costs. The combination of these factors means that what might trigger a buy or sell transaction in the institutional market often should be interpreted as a much more cautious 'hold' position by the private investor.

Styles of institutional fund management

Asset management has its own language and it is helpful to understand the tactical and strategic techniques they employ on your behalf. Never be afraid to ask questions and remember that one of the chief characteristics of stockbroking firms and fund management companies is a high ratio of ego to square footage of office space. It is not always backed by genuine intelligence, common sense and honesty, as the frequent investment scandals demonstrate.

The following descriptions are intended as a broad guide only, so at least you can bluff your way through the initial meetings.

Active managers

Don't expect active managers to look fit. Rich, yes, but not fit.

Active investment managers aim to increase a fund's value by deviating from a specific benchmark – for example a stockmarket index. There are two basic techniques used in active stock selection.

The starting point for active managers who adopt a 'bottom-up' approach is the company in which the manager may invest. The manager will look at in-house and external research on the company's history and potential future prospects. This will include an examination of the strength of the balance sheet, the company's trading history, the management's business strategy and the price/earnings ratio (the market price of a share divided by the company's earnings/profits per share in its latest 12-month trading period).

From the company analysis the manager will proceed to look at the general performance and prospects for that sector (for example construction, food retailers and so on) and then take into consideration national and international economic factors.

The 'top-down' manager works in reverse, looking first at the international and national economic factors that might affect economic growth in a country, geographic area (for example the 'Tiger' economies of South-east Asia) or economic category (emerging markets, for example) and gradually work down to the individual companies.

Active managers also have a style. For

example, 'value' managers seek out under-researched companies with potential. Some of the biggest names in institutional fund management have underperformed in recent years, partly because managers with this philosophy tend to avoid the biggest FTSE-100 companies if they appear overpriced – yet the FTSE-100 is where the main market growth has occurred.

Passive managers

Passive managers are, as the name suggests, pretty unassertive and can bore for Europe on subjects like index tracking through stratification as opposed to full replication.

Index tracking may sound simple, but in practice this is a complex process based on emulating the performance of a particular stockmarket index by buying all (full replication) or a sample (stratification) of the constituent shares.

The passive manager does not consider the merits of each stock, of different sectors and of economic cycles. If it is in the index then it must be represented in the fund. To date, index-tracking funds have done very well compared with actively managed funds, largely because the passive manager's charges are very low.

Quantitative management is like passive management with attitude. This is where the process tries to outstrip the index returns by deviating in a specific way. You can go through life without knowing anything about quant management.

That was a recommendation, not a statement.

Summary

- 'Securities' refers to UK equities, overseas equities, gilts and bonds.

- If a company wants to raise finance it can issue shares, which represent a share in the ownership, or bonds, which are a form of debt and behave like a sophisticated IOU.

- If you want to match or beat inflation, historically you would have had to invest in equities.

- Inflation has a major impact on the real return provided by your investments.

- Equities are only suitable for the medium to long term, due to their volatility and the cost of investing.

chapter 11

Nightmare on Wall Street

If you see a banker jump out of the window, jump after him – there's sure to be a profit in it.

Voltaire

After reading this chapter you will:

- buy a piggy bank;

- still want to buy and sell shares, despite the warning;

- feel very confused.

Savings and investments are a minefield. Unless you are really sure of your ability to pick funds it is wise to seek independent financial advice. Unfortunately, the market for financial advisers is also a minefield, but we provide some guidance for choosing a winner in Appendix 1.

Rainy days and Mondays

Everyone needs an immediate-access emergency fund to pay for unforeseen events such as sudden repairs on the car. However, this is not a role for mainstream investments such as unit or investment trusts. If you have to pull out of a longer term investment in a hurry you could lose money, particularly if there are setting up costs or exit charges.

The traditional home for cash is the deposit account. Check *Moneyfacts* (*see* page 30) for the best rates and remember you are not limited to building societies – there are lots of different companies in this market now, including supermarkets and insurance companies. You can also find useful information on the best rates for a variety of savings accounts in the personal finance pages of the weekend newspapers.

Avoid the common mistake of keeping too large a reserve when part of your money could be earning a potentially better return elsewhere. The size of your emergency fund should be determined by your monthly expenditure, your liabilities and the level of 'padding' you feel is appropriate for your lifestyle and peace of mind.

As a very rough guide it is worth keeping three times your monthly outgoings in an account that has one week's notice. Accounts offering a higher rate of interest with, say, three months' notice, can be used for known future capital expenditure – for example a new car or a holiday. You will find that postal and Internet accounts usually provide the best rates, particularly where they allow a limited number of withdrawals per annum. Interest rates are also tiered, so the more you put on deposit the higher the return.

If you manage your cashflow carefully then you can feed money from your other investments to your high-interest-rate account well in advance of the dates these more substantial bills fall due. Do keep a regular check on your longer term deposits, as rates change frequently.

An alternative to deposits is National Savings, which offer a wide range of accounts and bonds designed for every age and tax status. One of the attractions of NS products is that you can buy them through your local post office and there are no charges. Bear in mind though that NS interest rate change less frequently than building societies so you should always compare rates before committing yourself.

For details of the complete range of NS products ask at your local post office or use the contact details provided at the end of this chapter. Remember, NS does not pay commission to advisers – which may explain why many commission-based advisers fail to recommend these products.

> **Mean money**
> As a very rough guide it is worth keeping three times your monthly outgoings in an account that has one week's notice.

Collective funds

Unless you have just robbed a bank or a rich granny has died leaving you everything, stick to collective funds – for example unit trusts – where your money invests in a range of equities in order to spread risk. Buying and selling individual shares may look like a cool pastime but by all accounts you need about £100,000 to buy a decent spread of equities to diversify and reduce risk. Also, the costs of buying and selling are uneconomic for small portfolios.

In practice, many investors hold individual shares because they belong to an employee share option scheme at work, or they received free shares when their building society or life assurance company demutualized. Some

> Stand and deliver, **your** money
>
> or **your** wife …
>
> **On** second thoughts,
>
> we'll **just** take the **money**.

Colin Magruder, *The Sweeney* (1975)

employers and financial institutions offer cheap dealing facilities for their own shares.

For most people, the biggest long-term investments are earmarked for some specific purpose – for example, to repay your mortgage, to pay school fees for your children and to provide an income in retirement. However, it is important not to compartmentalize these investments but to include them in the overall portfolio planning.

This chapter looks at the main choices of collective funds. The most popular types of collective funds in the UK are unit trusts, open-ended investment companies and insurance company bonds. Also popular but slightly higher in risk profile are investment trusts. All of these funds offer a broad investment scope. Your choice will depend on the finer details.

Tax-efficient investments

Ironically, one of the main problems you are likely to encounter with collective funds is that there are far too many. You can hold many types of fund in a tax-efficient wrapper like a pension plan or individual savings account (Isa). Tax-efficient vehicles do not offer a magical solution to investment performance. What they do offer, however, is a shelter from income tax, capital gains tax, or both. If you run your own pension plan or Isa then you can invest in most asset classes and the returns will be enhanced due to the tax breaks.

The selection process

When it comes to selecting a good fund, there is plenty of advice on what not to do and very little on positive selection criteria, so what follows is to some extent subjective. No doubt over the years you will develop your own pet theories.

The financial press and several firms of consultants produce annual surveys that highlight the best and worst in the various categories of funds. You must take great care when you examine past performance statistics because these can be very misleading. What the surveys do offer, however, are some ideas on how to screen funds, so it is well worth checking out the methodology used in the most authoritative examples.

> **Mean money**
> Isas are most commonly used as a tax shelter for collective equity-based funds such as unit and investment trusts, but you can also put some money in deposits and life assurance funds.

There's a lot of disagreement about the use of past performance statistics but these can be a useful indicator *provided* you bear in mind the following important caveats:

- they must be coupled with a clear understanding of how past performance was achieved;
- they must be combined with an assessment of the current investment style of the management team;
- the individuals responsible for past performance must still be in place.

You also have to consider the level of risk taken to achieve those returns and whether you are comfortable with greater potential volatility in return. Size is important too. Some advisers recommend you avoid funds under £20 million because they have insufficient scope for diversification.

A good investment manager should be able to demonstrate a clear, measurable investment objective, which is set and met by the management team.

Individual savings accounts

Isas are the main tax-efficient investment apart from pensions (*see* Chapter 15). They were launched in April 1999 when they replaced personal equity plans (Peps) and tax-exempt special savings accounts (Tessas).

Isas are most commonly used as a tax shelter for collective equity-based funds such as unit and investment trusts, but you can also put some money in deposits and life assurance funds.

Here are the rules:

- £5,000 maximum annual contribution (£7,000 in 2000–1) including up to £1,000 of this in deposits/unit trust money market funds/National Savings, and £1,000 in life assurance funds;
- you can choose one company to manage the entire annual allowance for all the different components (known as a maxi Isa) or you can choose different managers for different components – maxi Isas are considered more flexible if you are unsure how much you want to invest in each component as the mini-Isa route can be restrictive;

- the fund is exempt from income tax and capital gains tax (although you must declare income and gains on your tax return);

- withdrawals can be made at any time without loss of tax relief (however providers may impose their own exit penalties);

- you can only have one Isa a year, although you can choose different managers for different tax years (but watch out for doubling up on charges);

- Isas from previous tax years can be switched to a new manager (this has to be for the whole fund, though, not just part).

Mean money

Unit trusts, with the exception of the index trackers, are generally considered slightly more expensive than investment trusts, but where the investment aims are similar, unit trusts are less sensitive to market movements.

For the equity component of the Isa there is a wide range of options, including ordinary shares, fixed-interest and convertible preference shares, corporate bonds (with at least five years to maturity), unit and investment trusts, and open-ended investment companies.

Unit trusts

A unit trust is a collection of shares and/or bonds with a specific investment aim. The trust can, for example, aim to produce an income by investing in high-yielding UK equities and/or corporate bonds. Or it could aim to generate capital growth by investing in new or expanding industries or, more riskily, in emerging markets.

Unit trusts sold to the public are authorized by the chief financial services regulator, the Financial Services Authority (FSA). You may hear about another type – 'unauthorized' unit trusts – which are used as internal funds by financial institutions and are not marketed to the public. Unit trusts are 'open ended', which means they may create or cancel units on a daily basis depending on demand.

As an investor you purchase units in the fund, and the value of these units fluctuates directly in line with the value of the underlying assets. In this respect a unit trust functions in a similar way to other collective funds – insurance company bonds for example – although the tax treatment for these two types of fund is quite different (*see* page 141).

Investment scope of unit trusts

Unit trust managers are free to decide which markets are suitable for their funds but they

October is **one** of the peculiarly **dangerous** months to **speculate** in stocks. The others are July, January, **September**, April, November, May ...

Mark Twain

must ensure the markets operate regularly, are open to the public and offer appropriate levels of liquidity.

Most funds invest mainly or wholly in equities, although the number of corporate bond funds, which invest in corporate bonds, preference shares and convertibles, among other assets, is growing rapidly. There are also gilt funds. Some advisers reckon it is comparatively easy and cheaper to select the right types of gilts for your circumstances direct from the National Savings Stock Register (NSSR). The main drawbacks with the NSSR are that you have to deal by post and there are limits on the maximum size of transactions.

Some unit trusts offer capital guarantees or guarantee to provide part of the rise in a stockmarket index and protect you from the falls. The guarantee is 'insured' through the use of certain types of derivatives – financial instruments that can be used to protect a fund's exposure to market fluctuations.

Always remember that guarantees carry a cost – in this case the price of the derivatives – which will be passed on to the investor. Some

advisers argue that you might be better off gaining full exposure to a stockmarket index through one of the low-cost index-tracking unit trusts and limiting your exposure to risk by investing part of your capital in gilts or National Savings Certificates, for example.

Open-ended investment companies

To all intents and purposes you can regard open-ended investment companies (oeics, pronounced 'oiks') as similar to unit trusts. For the technically minded, oeics have a corporate structure and combine characteristics of both unit and investment trusts. For example, they can have different classes of share, which offer different features. In this respect they offer some of the flexibility of split-capital investment trusts, which allow investors to take maximum income at the expense of capital growth, and those seeking growth to take maximum growth at the expense of income.

Oeics do not have a different selling and buying price, unlike the complicated 'bid/offer spread' of unit trusts (you sell at the bid price and buy at the offer price – the difference represents the seller's profit). Instead they have just one mid-market price – literally the mid-point between the bid/offer spread – at which investors both buy and sell.

It may not be easy to compare the performance of oeics with unit trusts. This is because some of the charges for an oeic, as with an investment trust, are deducted from within the company, whereas with a unit trust the charges are separate from the trust itself.

As with qualifying unit trusts, qualifying oeics can be held in an Isa.

Investment trusts

An investment trust is not a trust as such but is a British company, listed on the UK Stock Exchange, which invests in the shares of other quoted and unquoted companies in the UK and overseas. It may also invest in fixed interest securities, cash or other assets. As public companies, investment trusts are subject to company law and Stock Exchange regulation. The prices of most investment trusts are published daily in the *Financial Times*.

Investment trusts are controlled by boards of directors who are appointed by and answerable to their shareholders. The board presents annual accounts to its shareholders.

The difference between investment and unit trusts

Investment trusts are different from unit trusts in several important ways and offer the active investor additional opportunities. However, these opportunities also make investment trusts potentially more volatile than unit trusts.

Investment trust companies have a fixed number of shares so, unlike unit trusts, 'units' cannot be created and cancelled to meet increased and reduced demand. As with any quoted company, the shares are only available when other investors are trying to sell. This means there are two factors that affect investment trust share prices. The first is the performance of the underlying assets in which the company invests. This factor also affects the price of units in a unit trust.

However, where unit trust prices directly reflect the net asset value (the market price of securities held in the fund), investment trust share prices may not. This leads to the second factor, which is that the market forces (supply and demand) to which investment trust shares are subject may make the shares worth more or less than the underlying value of the company's assets. If the share price is lower than the value of the underlying assets the difference is known as the discount. If it is higher the difference is known as the premium.

Investment trusts can borrow money to invest – an activity known as gearing. This adds extra flexibility and if the shares purchased with the borrowed money do well, the company and its shareholders will benefit. Conversely, a poor return on the shares will reduce the profitability of the company.

Split-capital investment trusts can have several types of shares, but generally offer two principal categories. One has a right to all the income and the other has a right to the capital growth. There are several other types of share, each offering different features. An example is a stepped-preference share which offers dividends that rise at a predetermined rate, and a fixed redemption value that is paid when the trust is wound up.

Investment-trust warrants also offer the active investor the right to subscribe to new shares at a certain price, on a certain date. Typically, an investment trust might have one warrant for every five ordinary shares. It is important to check how many warrants are in circulation because if the investors holding these instruments decide to exercise their

right, this will effectively dilute existing ordinary shareholders' rights because the net asset value is divided by a greater number of shares.

Unit and investment trusts: taxation and charges

In terms of taxation, the unit and investment trust route is very similar. Where these investments are held outside an Isa, the capital gains tax liability falls on the investor, who can offset it against the annual CGT exemption (*see* page 77).

Dividends are paid net of lower rate tax. This can be reclaimed by non-taxpayers but there would be a potential additional 20 per cent liability for higher rate payers. Where funds are qualifying, both types of trust may be held in an Isa, in which case income and gains are tax free.

Remember, though, that the advantage of a capital gains tax shelter can become a disadvantage if the fund makes a capital loss because this loss cannot be offset against any gains made during a tax year in excess of the CGT exemption.

Charges on investment trusts are generally lower than on unit trusts, with the exception of index trackers. However, tracker funds are usually confined to the UK stockmarket and therefore do not offer such broad diversification as the larger and older international investment trusts.

Mean money
Always remember that guarantees carry a cost – in this case the price of derivatives – which will be passed on to the investor.

In conclusion, unit trusts, with the exception of the index trackers, are generally considered slightly more expensive than investment trusts, but where the investment aims are similar, unit trusts are less sensitive to market movements.

Insurance company bonds

Like unit trusts, a lump sum premium in an insurance company bond buys units that directly reflect the net asset value of the fund's underlying investments.

The charges for the two types of collective funds are similar. However, the tax treatment is quite different. Insurance company bonds pay tax broadly equivalent to the lower rate on income and capital gains. The income tax cannot be reclaimed so, generally, these bonds are not considered suitable for non-taxpayers. Moreover, the capital gains tax paid by the fund cannot be offset against an individual's exemption. Advisers tend to regard this feature as a drawback although the range of funds can be attractive to lower risk investors.

Offshore funds

There is a huge range of offshore funds run out of the Channel Islands, the Isle of Man, the Dublin International Financial Centre and Luxembourg. (There are other offshore centres but those mentioned are of most relevance to the UK market.)

The appeal of offshore funds for UK residents will depend on the tax jurisdiction of the fund and the way the fund itself is taxed (in particular, whether it distributes its income or rolls it up in the fund). It will also depend on your own tax position as an investor. For non-UK residents offshore vehicles can be very attractive, but their merits are questionable for UK residents. Either way, expert advice is essential.

Additional points to consider with offshore funds include the charges, which are usually much higher than UK funds, and the regulation. It the fund is based outside the UK, do check very carefully what protection you have if the company collapses or the fund manager runs off with your money.

As a general rule for a UK resident investing in UK securities, unit and investment trusts are likely to prove more cost effective and simpler than offshore funds.

In addition to the offshore unit trusts and their foreign equivalents, there are two main types of offshore insurance bond – distribution bonds, which pay a regular 'income', and non-distribution bonds, which roll up gross.

Investors who may gain by going offshore include UK and foreign expatriates who are non-resident for UK tax purposes and who can benefit from gross roll-up non-distribution bonds if they do not pay tax in the country where they live. Higher rate taxpayers may also benefit from the gross roll up but you do have to pay tax when you bring the money back into the UK, although of course you may have switched to the lower tax bracket if you have retired by the time the non-distribution bond matures.

It is worth noting that the government frowns on the use of offshore funds and trusts to avoid or minimize your tax liability, so in future there may be changes to tighten up any loopholes.

Summary

- Set your investment goals before you consider in which tax-efficient vehicle you should place certain assets.

- Past performance statistics are an imperfect guide to the future, but can help if you follow the methodology used by the professional consultants' surveys.

- Check that the management group that achieved the performance is still in place and has a clearly defined, measurable investment objective for the fund in which you are interested.

- The structure of investment trusts offers greater investment opportunities but at the same time greater potential risk than unit trusts.

- For most investors, unit and investment trusts are more tax efficient than insurance company bonds.

- Open-ended investment companies are said to combine the best features of unit and investment trusts, but are too new to have proved their mettle.

- Unless there is a very good reason, UK residents will find onshore funds cheaper and simpler than their offshore equivalent.

chapter 12

Farewell

to arms

Look boss, I only **got**
one rule. And that's
never bet **money**
you **don't have**
on a dog race **with**
an ex-girlfriend **who**
happens **to be** a stripper.

Romeo Posar, *Tin Cup* (1996)

After reading this chapter you will:

- still want your aunt to leave you her mink coat in her will;

- get rich by investing in illegal drug trafficking, guns and gambling;

- support the right to arm bears.

If you ask ten people what they think is ethical you will get ten different answers. Ethical views, by their very nature, are subjective. Nevertheless, in this chapter we consider how, as an investor, you can put your ethical and environmental views into practice. If you have any, that is.

As an ethical investor you will have to use your personal opinions to decide which companies are worth investing in and which should be shunned. Whether you make your own selections or you wish to set guidelines for your financial adviser, it is important to be able to explain your views clearly.

You also need to appreciate the impact any ethical screening process will have on a fund's annual returns. An ethical fund will not have broad exposure to the FTSE All-Share index, for example, which is the benchmark used to judge the performance of most general equity funds. An ethical fund, therefore, needs to have an appropriate performance benchmark and should not be expected to reflect market movements as a whole.

Bear in mind that some advisers are much more sympathetic than others when it comes to ethical investment. An adviser who takes the matter seriously will have considerable research at his or her disposal. A cynic will probably try to dissuade you, pointing out the significant constraints on the choice of shares and how this can undermine performance.

Don't dismiss the cynical approach.

Remember, any strong ethical views you may have are likely to go against your adviser's natural instinct to help you make as much money as possible.

Ethical Investment Research Service

Ethical investment is a complicated subject and is not helped by the difficulty and cost of obtaining sufficient data upon which to form a view about the ethics or otherwise of a company. A good source of information for people interested in this subject is the Ethical Investment Research Service (EIRIS), which maintains a database of ethical funds and individual companies.

EIRIS was set up in 1983 by a number of organizations including the Society of Friends (Quakers), Methodists, Oxfam and the Rowntree Trust. It monitors the screening and performance of the ethical and environmental unit trusts, so if you are interested in collective funds, this is the best place to start.

It also offers a screening process for direct-equity investors. The simplest way to use EIRIS research is to request an 'acceptable list' – a list of companies that meet your ethical or environmental criteria. A 'portfolio screen'

Let me see if I've got this straight:
in order to be grounded
I've got to be crazy
and I must be crazy to keep flying.
But if I ask to be grounded,
that means I'm not crazy any more
and I have to keep flying.

Yossarian, *Catch22* (1970)

enables you to find out more about the shares you hold, while for the real enthusiast, EIRIS factsheets provide all the information on the database on the companies in question (*see* page 152).

EIRIS researches over 1,000 companies. The list of screening options from which you can choose gives you an idea of why this is such a complicated topic:

- alcohol
- animals (meat production and sale, leather/fur manufacture and sale)
- arms and sales to military purchasers
- community involvement
- corporate governance
- directors' pay
- environmental issues
- equal opportunities
- gambling
- greenhouse gases
- health and safety convictions
- human rights
- intensive farming
- military contracts
- newspaper production and television
- nuclear power (fuel, components and construction of plants)
- overseas interests (wages exploitation in emerging economies, deriving profits from

countries with poor human rights records)
- ozone-depleting chemicals
- pesticides
- political contributions
- pornography
- Third World involvement
- tropical hardwood
- tobacco
- waste disposal
- water pollution.

Mean money

The major exclusions in ethical funds tend to be arms, alcohol, tobacco, gambling, animal testing, environmental damage and the payment of exploitative wages in developing countries.

Defining an ethical policy

The major exclusions in ethical funds tend to be arms, alcohol, tobacco, gambling, animal testing, environmental damage and the payment of exploitative wages in developing countries. But the list could extend almost indefinitely.

Some funds take a proactive approach and aim to invest in companies that are working towards a desirable goal – 'green' companies involved in recycling or environmentally friendly waste disposal, for example. Environmental funds can also be regarded as ethical. Here the choice of shares will depend on a company's environmental policy in terms of pollution, ozone depletion, deforestation and waste management, among other criteria.

If you have strong ethical views you need to decide where to draw the line. It is one thing to exclude tobacco and/or alcohol companies, but what about the supermarkets that sell their products? Think carefully before you exclude companies which employ 'children' in developing countries – in some societies adulthood starts at the age of 12.

> **Mean money**
> It is one thing to exclude tobacco and/or alcohol companies, but what about the supermarkets that sell their products?

Gambling is also a typical exclusion, but does this mean all the outlets that sell tickets for the National Lottery should be avoided? Some

ethical investors might favour pharmaceutical companies because of their groundbreaking research in the war against cancer and AIDS, for example. Others might exclude the same companies on the grounds that they carry out experiments on animals.

In an extreme case, even apparently innocuous products like National Savings and gilts can cause problems because they are effectively 'sold' by the UK government. The same government is responsible for the massive expenditure on arms and animal experiments, via public and private sector agencies and universities. You must decide whether these factors outweigh the benefits of expenditure on education, health and social security.

Broad-brush approach

In practice, many investors settle for a broad-brush approach that eliminates the obvious villains but does not go into too much detail. Using the analogy above, this would exclude the tobacco companies but not the supermarkets that sell cigarettes. This approach would also screen out the companies whose primary business is armaments, but could leave you with companies with a minority interest in arms.

Probably some element of compromise is called for, but you have to decide how far you are prepared to go to identify the ethical stars and whether you are prepared to accept the resulting restriction in investment choice. If

Look, all I know is what they taught me at command school. There are certain rules about war and rule number one is young men die. And rule number two is doctors can't change rule number one.

Henry Blake, *M*A*S*H* (1972)

you take ethical investment to its natural conclusion you will end up investing purely in property. This is not a good idea.

You also need to decide whether to limit your ethical investment views to your private portfolio of shares and funds or whether to take it further. For example, if you are in a company pension scheme, what influence, if any, can you have over the investment aims of the pension fund? The chances are, this would be limited to your freedom to express your views to the trustees. Ultimately, you could decide to leave the scheme and set up your own ethical personal pension plan, but this could be a very high price to pay because the company scheme is a very valuable benefit for you and your dependants (see Chapter 14).

The impact of ethical screening on performance

Critics of ethical investment argue that performance suffers due to the exclusion of many major FTSE-100 companies, most of which include something distinctly unethical somewhere among their diverse operations.

If a fund excludes the very obvious unethical villains it would lose access to about 8 per cent of the stockmarket by value. This figure grows if you add animal testing, nuclear power, and environmental damage, for example. The full EIRIS screening, shown above, disqualifies up to 60 per cent of the FTSE-100 companies.

This means that an ethical fund is likely to have a disproportionate weighting towards smaller, more risky companies. As far as performance goes, smaller companies have the ability to outperform their larger counterparts. But they are also inclined to be more volatile and must be selected with great care, as the performance of the FTSE-250 and SmallCap (the smallest 550 or so in the FTSE All-Share index) have demonstrated over the past few years. Bear in mind that when the SmallCap does well it is often due to the stunning outperformance of a handful of companies rather than a consistently good performance across the board.

In addition, there is a danger that the ethical policy leaves a fund overexposed to certain sectors that may only be ethical by default – the hotels and leisure industry, for example. Moreover, the fund would be unable to reap the rewards of a boom in other sectors such as chemicals, engineering or pharmaceuticals.

A good year to examine in this context is 1997, when most general ethical funds underperformed the market as a whole because they had limited exposure to the sectors that outperformed. Typical exclusions that proved regrettable from the performance point of view included banks (most lend money indiscriminately to non-ethical companies and countries with poor human rights records), integrated oils (environmental damage) and pharmaceuticals (animal testing and, occasionally, exploitation in tests on humans in emerging countries).

Alternative investments

EIRIS provides details of investments that it believes offer a distinct social value but which are not listed on the Stock Exchange. Examples include investment in a company that imports tropical hardwood from sustainable sources, or one involved in fair trade with developing economies.

> ## Mean money
> An ethical policy may leave a fund overexposed to certain sectors that are only ethical by default – the hotels and leisure industry, for example.

The attraction here is that by investing in these companies you help them to grow. However, the downside is that the shares may not pay dividends and can be difficult to sell. Moreover, all the usual warnings about small companies apply with a vengeance.

Summary

- Ethical views are very subjective so it is essential you give your stockbroker a clear mandate on exclusions.

- Decide if you want to screen in a positive manner or simply to eliminate the main culprits.

- Use the EIRIS screening service to draw up your list of acceptable companies.

- Be aware that an ethical portfolio will usually consist mainly of small to medium-sized companies.

Further information

Money and Ethics, a guide to collective funds is available from EIRIS. Also available from EIRIS are a guide to financial advisers who offer advice on ethical investments and a guide to fund managers and stockbrokers who manage portfolios with ethical constraints. Contact EIRIS, 504 Bondway Business Centre, 71 Bondway, London SW8 1SQ.

Life and Pensions Moneyfacts lists ethical and environmental life assurance and pension funds plus unit trusts. Contact *Moneyfacts*, Moneyfacts House, 66–70 Thorpe Road, Norwich NR1 1BJ (01603 476476).

The UK Social Investment Forum website provides lots of useful details on ethical investment: www.uksif.org.site

chapter 13

The
tax man
cometh

A man **must** know
the **right occasion**
to
indulge
in tax evasion.

Harry Weiss, *Shock Treatment* (1981)

After reading this chapter you will:

- realize that tax evasion can be fun, if a tad risky;

- explain to your parents why it's cool tax planning for them to give you their shares;

- wonder how accountants ever get anyone to go to bed with them.

Smart tax saving begins at home. Here you can redistribute income and assets to make best use of each family member's annual personal allowances and exemptions. You should also consider making appropriate inheritance tax arrangements to help retain your wealth within the family when you die.

However, do not use your quota just for the sake of it. First look at how much tax you will save and find out if this is negated by complicated and expensive administration, as might be the case where you have to set up a trust.

Also, do bear in mind that security and peace of mind are important. Gifts made to avoid tax must be unconditional, otherwise the Revenue will see through the arrangement and continue to assess you on their value. Tax efficiency aside, you may rue the day you gave your favourite shares to your spouse.

The basics of income tax and national insurance are explained in Chapter 6, and Table 6.1 on page 72 shows the main tax rates, allowances and exemptions. For more specific details consult your accountant or the Inland Revenue. This chapter summarizes the most important allowances and exemptions that do not require expensive and complicated arrangements. All figures are for the 2000–1 tax year.

Keep it legal

The hallmark of good tax planning is that it will pass the Inland Revenue's scrutiny with flying colours, even where complicated family trust arrangements and considerable wealth are involved.

The Inland Revenue distinguishes between our various attempts to minimize our tax liability. In particular you need to understand the terms 'evasion', 'avoidance' and 'mitigation'. Although these tend to be used indiscriminately, their meanings are *very* different.

If you deliberately omit something from your tax return, or give a false description, that's evasion. You have not just been dishonest – you have acted criminally and could be fined or imprisoned.

Mean money
The hallmark of good tax planning is that it will pass the Inland Revenue's scrutiny with flying colours.

Avoidance and mitigation, by contrast, are on the right side of the law but again, there is an important distinction. If your tax saving has been encouraged by the government – for example you put your investments in an individual savings account (Isa) – that is mitigation and is definitely on the right side of the Revenue.

By contrast, avoidance involves saving tax by using certain loopholes in the law. This is not

Victims? Don't be melodramatic, Holly. Look down there. Would you really feel any pity if one of those dots stopped moving – forever? If I said you could have £20,000 for every dot that stops, would you really, old man, tell me to keep my money – without hesitation? Or would you calculate how many dots you could afford to spare? Free of income tax, old man. Free of income tax. It's the only way to save nowadays.

Harry Lime, *The Third Man* (1949)

illegal, but such loopholes exist only because the Inland Revenue hasn't yet got around to closing them or because to do so would create an impossibly complex set of rules.

Among other services, your accountants will help you to mitigate and avoid tax.

Your tax allowances and exemptions

Successful tax planning requires common sense and expert advice, in equal measures. So, before you change anything, check that the particular use of an allowance or exemption has a genuine benefit. In some cases the cost of setting up and maintaining the arrangement can outweigh any tax savings. Unless you are very experienced, do consult a qualified accountant. All transactions must comply with current tax law and be carefully documented.

There are three main personal allowances and exemptions. A full set of figures is provided in Table 6.1, but briefly, for the 2000–1 tax year, each member of your family has:

- the income tax annual personal allowance of £4,385 (more if you qualify for the married couple's and/or the age allowances)
- the capital gains tax annual exemption of £7,200
- the inheritance tax annual exemption for

gifts of £3,000. The main exemption on death is £234,000.

Income tax

Most families are not tax efficient because their combined wealth – both in terms of earned income and assets – tends to be concentrated in the hands of the main breadwinner. He or she, therefore, is also responsible for paying most of the tax, usually at the top rate.

One of the best ways to save on income tax is to share income between spouses, whether the source is earnings, investments or a combination of the two. This makes use of the non-working or lower earning spouse's allowance and, where the income exceeds the personal allowance, the lower and basic tax rates. The two most common redistribution techniques are to give income-generating assets to your spouse and, where you run your own business, to pay your spouse a salary.

Mean money
The terms 'evasion', 'avoidance' and 'mitigation' tend to be used indiscriminately, but their meanings are *very* different.

Mean money

Do not use your tax allowance and exemptions just for the sake of it. First look at how much tax you will save and find out if this is negated by complicated and expensive administration.

It is also possible to give income-producing assets to children who can make use of their own allowances and, where necessary, their lower and basic rates of taxation. However, this requires great care. If you give this type of asset to your children and the income exceeds £100 per annum, you, as the parents, will be taxed on the entire amount. For this reason usually it is necessary to hold the assets in a 'bare trust' under which the parents are the registered owners but hold them as nominees for the children. The income is accumulated until the children are 18. This would not be necessary in the case of gifts from other family members – grandparents, for example.

Finally on this point, do remember that if you give a gift of assets this has to be unconditional, otherwise the Revenue will see through the arrangement and continue to tax you on the asset's value. Think carefully before you give your favourite shares to your spouse or children!

Capital gains tax

The annual exemption of £7,200 for the 2000–1 tax year is the amount of capital gains you can make before you pay capital gains tax (CGT) at your top rate of income tax. As gifts between spouses are exempt from CGT, the tax-efficient couple should consider sharing assets in order to make use of both exemptions.

CGT and your shares

In practice most investors manage to avoid CGT without making any special arrangements, simply because their liability regularly falls within the annual CGT exemption. Even if you have a very large portfolio and you are an active investor, you may still be able to avoid or reduce your liability, but this will require some careful planning.

CGT is payable when you sell an asset and make a 'chargeable gain', that is, where the value of an asset you sell has increased since you acquired it, after taking into account the effect of inflation. Remember, CGT is not charged on the asset itself but on its gain in value.

Inheritance tax

Inheritance tax (IHT) is a tax on your wealth at death and is deducted from your estate before it can be passed on to your heirs. There is no

Why, this whole country is run on epidemics … Where you been? Big business, price fixing, crooked TV shows, income tax finagling, souped up expense accounts. How many honest men do you know?

Hud Bannon, *Hud* (1963)

IHT liability on the assets you leave to your spouse, but once he or she dies, then the value of the estate in excess of the exemption is taxable.

There are several ways to mitigate your inheritance tax bill. Each year you can give away up to £3,000 free of CGT. If you didn't use last year's exemption you can add it to this year's, giving a total gift of £12,000 per couple.

It is possible to give away any amount in excess of this but at present, if you die within seven years, you pay tax on a sliding scale based on when you made the gift and when you die. This arrangement, known as a 'potentially exempt transfer' (PET), may be abolished in a future Budget along with other IHT-avoidance measures.

Summary

- Make sure your tax arrangements are not so complicated that they eliminate any tax savings in administration costs.

- Where possible, married couples should share assets to make use of both partners' personal income tax allowance and capital gains tax exemption. This is particularly tax efficient if one partner is a non-taxpayer or pays tax at the lower or basic rate.

- A capital loss can be offset against any capital gains in excess of the exemption.

The long goodbye

Well, look at me. I'm old, lacking in vigour, my mind's in a turmoil. I no longer know if I'm coming, have gone or even been. I'm falling to pieces; I no longer even have any clothes sense.

The Doctor, *Doctor Who* (1963)

[Still from *Kind Hearts and Coronets*, Canal+Image UK Ltd]

Gold
watch
blues

Mom **started** borrowing

my clothes. There

should

be an **age limit** on lycra

pants. And dad, **he just**

locked himself in the

bathroom with **old**

copies of *Esquire*.

Cordelia, *Buffy the Vampire Slayer*
(1997)

After reading this chapter you will:

- love your pension scheme even if you don't understand it;

- treat actuaries with more respect;

- know that when your employer replaces your scheme with something 'simpler and more flexible', it's to save the company money.

State pension? Forget it!

The UK has one of the most complex state pension schemes in Europe. It also pays out one of the lowest levels of benefit. Over the next two decades the complexities will increase, while the pensions paid will be cut even further.

There is no point in dwelling on state pensions. If you are under 30, by the time you retire the chances are that any state earnings-related pension (Serps) entitlement will have been withdrawn and the flat-rate old age pension will be means tested. It's a chilling scenario but at least it may focus your mind on making your own provision.

Eligibility to state pensions is built up through the compulsory payment of national insurance (NI) contributions on part of your earnings. National insurance is explained on page 71.

Company pension schemes

The UK has the most developed private pensions system in the European Union. Over 11 million employees and their families rely on company pension schemes, which in turn are backed by assets worth over £750 billion.

For the vast majority of employees, membership of the company pension scheme represents the most important benefit after the salary itself. For a start, company schemes are tax efficient. The employer's contributions are tax deductible, the employee's contributions are paid free of basic and higher rate tax, the pension fund builds up virtually tax free and a significant chunk of the final benefits can be taken as tax-free cash at retirement. The pension itself is taxed as income.

Today more employees understand the nature of their schemes and the value of these benefits than in the past. But there are still many who fail to look beyond the monthly deductions from their pay cheque and naively assume that their employer will see them right. This is tantamount to leaving your financial security in retirement to luck. Some schemes provide very good pensions while others will barely provide a subsistence income. The trick is knowing how to spot the difference and what to do if your scheme falls into the skimpy category.

Industry-wide and 'stakeholder' schemes

Occupational pensions are not limited to single-employer schemes. An increasing number of employers belong to industry-wide arrangements where a scheme is set up to cater for all employees within a specific sector – for example broadcasting, civil engineering, the voluntary sector, hotels and leisure groups, and so on.

The government plans to extend the availability of such schemes through 'stakeholder' pensions, so that employees and the self-employed who do not have access to

a company pension can still join a group scheme. This initiative, which should come into force in April 2001, is very welcome.

Group arrangements generally offer economies of scale that cannot be achieved by individual plans and are therefore much better value. Stakeholders will be a special type of industry-wide scheme that will meet certain government guidelines on charges, flexibility and terms. Many existing industry-wide schemes already broadly meet these requirements.

If your company does not offer its own pension scheme then it makes sense to consider an industry-wide or, in due course, a stakeholder scheme. Ask your trade union or professional body for information. If there is nothing available at present, then take out a personal pension but make sure it is totally flexible so that you are not tied to this individual plan if something better comes along at a later date.

How occupational schemes work

Despite the complicated rules and regulations, the basic principles of company schemes are really quite straightforward. However, you may have to persevere if you want to get clear information out of your pensions manager or trustees. A spot of background knowledge will stand you in good stead. But first, consider the facts and figures in Table 14.1.

Mean money

The state scheme only pays pensions to 'lawful spouses'. This is nothing to do with family values and everything to do with stinginess.

Trust law

Occupational pension schemes are based largely on trust law, but this framework was reinforced by statutory regulations introduced by the Pensions Act 1995. Trust law goes back to the Middle Ages, and is pretty quirky.

However, there are three good reasons for using trust law as the basis for pension schemes:

- to separate the pension fund from the rest of the company's assets – in theory this keeps the fund safe, for example from predators if the company is the subject of a hostile take-over or from creditors if the company goes bust;

- to manage money on behalf of others – in the case of a pension fund the money is managed on behalf of the scheme members and other beneficiaries who, for tax reasons, cannot get their hands on their pension until normal retirement date;

- to obtain Inland Revenue approval to qualify for tax purposes.

Table 14.1

Facts about company pensions
Number of employees covered by occupational schemes: 11 million plus their families
Total working population: 28 million, of which 23 million are employed
Total value of funds: £755 billion
Typical employee contribution rate: 5 per cent (final salary); 3.5 per cent (money purchase)
Percentage of schemes non-contributory: 24 per cent
Percentage of company schemes run on a money-purchase basis: 15–20 per cent
Percentage of schemes that can provide unmarried partners' pensions (at trustees' discretion): 66 per cent (private sector); 15 per cent (public sector)

Source: National Association of Pension Funds

Trustees and 'beneficiaries'

You can't have a trust without a trustee who, as legal owner of the fund, is obliged to look after the assets on behalf of the beneficiaries. In the case of pension funds the beneficiaries are:

- the scheme members;
- retired scheme members drawing pensions;
- ex-employees with deferred pensions (pension benefits they left behind when changing jobs);
- the dependants (spouses and children) of all three categories.

Historically, employers drew most of their trustees from the management team, but clearly this could, and sometimes did, lead to abuse. If the company was cash poor but pension fund rich it could be tempting for the management trustees to use the fund to bolster up the company's flagging finances.

To improve the balance of power on trustee boards, from April 1997 scheme members have the right (but not the obligation) to appoint one-third of the trustee board from their ranks. In practice, of course, their presence alone will make little difference if they do not understand the job. It requires a trained eye to spot pensions skulduggery in the making, so if you are thinking of becoming a member trustee be sure to insist on some proper training for the job.

Oh come on, thirty more years of this, you get a tiny pension and a cheap gold watch.

Harry Temple, *Speed* (1994)

Pensions Act (1995)

The Pensions Act, which came into force in April 1997, followed a widespread overhaul of pensions legislation in the wake of the Robert Maxwell scandal, when millions of pounds went missing from his company's pension

Mean money
With a final-salary scheme the investment risk and guarantees are backed by the employer. With a money-purchase scheme the investment risk falls fairly and squarely on your shoulders and there are no guarantees. Not surprisingly, money-purchase schems are providing very popular with employers.

fund. The legislation generally is aimed to improve the security of pension funds by introducing a new series of checks and balances, and by appointing a pensions regulator.

The main types of pension scheme

There are two main types of occupational schemes – 'final salary' (also known as 'defined benefit'), and 'money purchase' (also known as 'defined contribution'). With a final-salary scheme the investment risk and guarantees are backed by the employer. With a money-purchase scheme the investment risk falls fairly and squarely on your shoulders as the scheme member and there are no guarantees. Not surprisingly, money-purchase schemes are proving very popular with employers.

Final-salary schemes

Final-salary schemes, still the most prevalent among employers in the UK, base the pension calculation on the number of years of service and your salary at or near retirement. Rather oddly, for what is essentially a tax-efficient investment, this means there is no direct link between what you pay in and what you get out. This explains much of the confusion that arises with these schemes.

A typical scheme might guarantee to provide a pension that builds up at the rate of one-sixtieth of your final salary for each year of service up to an Inland Revenue maximum of forty-sixtieths – that is, two-thirds final salary at retirement (restricted for some higher earners).

In 1988 – the year personal pensions were introduced – companies lost the right to make membership of their schemes a condition of employment, although in most cases it will be in your best interests to join. Some companies operate an automatic membership system so if for some reason you don't want to join you have the right to opt out. The government is likely to reintroduce compulsory membership for employees in its bid to increase private pension coverage.

Employee contributions

Employees can contribute up to 15 per cent of gross pay to an occupational scheme, although the most common rate is about 5 per cent. The proportion of your earnings on which you can base your contributions will vary from scheme to scheme. Some schemes provide a pension linked to basic pay while others take into account the other elements that make up gross pay, including, for example, regular overtime or sales-related commission.

If overtime forms a significant proportion of your gross earnings and this is not taken into account in your pensionable pay, you could consider top up provision through additional voluntary contributions or some other tax-efficient investments.

Employer contributions

The employer's contributions are an extremely valuable perk. Where employers pay a fixed rate in a generous scheme this may be worth twice the value of the employees' contributions. In practice, however, employers tend to vary their contributions according to what the scheme actuary calculates must be invested so the fund can pay the pensions and benefits guaranteed by the scheme. As a result, employers tend to pay more on behalf of older employees approaching retirement than for younger employees who have 30–40 years to go.

Restrictions for higher earners

Over the past five years the Revenue has restricted the pensions of certain high earners. In particular, some employees are subject to a cap of £91,800 for the 2000–1 tax year, on which contributions and the final pension can be based.

Topping up your company pension

By law every scheme, with a few minor exceptions, must provide an additional voluntary contribution (AVC) scheme, which allows members to top up their company pension. In practice very few people end up

with the maximum permitted pension so most will benefit from AVCs.

Since 1987 employees also have been able to contribute to individual top-up plans known as free-standing AVCs (FSAVCs), which are sold by insurance companies and other financial institutions. As a general rule, however, the company AVC scheme will offer better value than an individual plan. You might also consider individual savings accounts (Isas) for retirement income planning (*see* page 137).

Contracting out

Most final-salary schemes are contracted out of the state earnings-related pension scheme (Serps). As a result, the employer and, in most cases, employees pay a reduced rate of national insurance contribution with the balance invested in the company pension fund. National insurance is a type of tax which most employees pay at the rate of 10

Mean money

The employers' contributions are an extremely valuable perk. Where employers pay a fixed rate in a generous scheme this may be worth twice the value of the employees' contributions and often much more.

Look, Lister, no point

feeling sorry about Holly.

It's a kindness.

Like an old, blind,

incontinent sheepdog,

he's had his day. Take him out to

the barn with a

double barrelled shot-gun

and blow the mother away.

And I'm only saying that because

I'm so fond of him. Rimmer, *Red Dwarf* (1988)

Tax-free cash

The maximum tax-free cash you can take from your company pension scheme is one-and-a-half times your final salary after 40 years service. This is limited in the case of some higher earners (*see* page 169). If you are in a private sector scheme and you take the tax-free cash, your pension will be reduced.

Pension increases

Most company schemes increase pensions by 3–5 per cent each year. However, you need to check which increases are guaranteed and which are not. Voluntary payments by the fund are known as 'discretionary' increases. Public-sector pensions automatically increase in line with inflation.

per cent on 'middle band earnings', that is earnings between £76 and £535 per week in 2000–1.

Where the scheme is not contracted out the employee would receive the Serps pension and the company pension on top of this. However, Serps is being phased out and in future unless you are on very low earnings you will be expected to find a stakeholder scheme to cover your basic pension requirements.

Family protection benefits

Final-salary schemes provide other important family protection benefits in addition to the pension itself, for example death-in-service benefits can be paid of up to four times annual salary (the typical rate is two or three times salary), a widow's or widower's pension, dependent children's pensions and similar death-in-retirement benefits. Disability pensions and private medical insurance are also common features of the overall benefits package.

Benefits for unmarried partners

Scheme members with unmarried partners, whether of the opposite or the same sex, are often the subject of discrimination if the scheme rules only permit death benefits and survivor pensions to be paid to the lawful spouse.

Usually it is possible to nominate the person to whom your death-in-service benefits should go and these nomination forms remain sealed until your death, so that gay and lesbian scheme members do not have to disclose details of their private lives.

Payment of the pension to anyone other than the lawful spouse is more difficult to arrange, although some schemes have introduced rules to allow partners' pensions to be paid to common-law spouses. Usually though, payment may only be made provided the relationship was long term and a significant degree of financial interdependency can be proved.

If you want to find out your position under your own scheme rules, look in the scheme booklet and if this is not clear, contact the trustees.

The state scheme only pays pensions to 'lawful spouses'. This has nothing to do with family values and everything to do with stinginess.

Pension fund investment

Under a final-salary scheme the employee and employer contributions go into a central trust fund that is legally separate from the assets owned and controlled by the company. The legal owners of the fund are the trustees who, as explained above, look after the assets on behalf of the beneficiaries.

The trustees are expected to delegate the day-to-day investment management to professionals. How well the fund performs often dictates the future level of contributions and benefits, particularly with regard to discretionary pension increases (increases that are not guaranteed by the scheme but which the trustees feel the fund is capable of paying).

Most large pension schemes are 'self-administered', which means that the fund management is separate from the administration . However, both functions can be carried out by specialists who work directly for the pension fund. Smaller schemes, and this includes many money-purchase schemes (see page 173), tend to be run by life offices, which offer a combined investment and administration service, although where the fund management is handled by a unit or investment trust group, a third party usually is appointed for the administration.

box 14.1
What a good final salary scheme might offer

- A pension of two-thirds final salary after a maximum of 40 years, not taking account of the state pension.
- Pension based on total earnings not just basic pay.
- Suitable arrangements for high earners whose pensionable salary is capped.*
- Annual pension increases in line with retail prices.
- Death-in-retirement pension for partner (not just the narrower definition of 'spouse') of two-thirds your own plus a pension for children under 18.
- Death-in-service pension for your partner and children under 18, plus a lump sum of three times annual salary (the Revenue maximum is four times salary).
- Ill-health pension equivalent to the amount you would have received if you had continued to retirement age at the same rate of pay.
- If you change jobs the whole of the 'preserved' pension you leave with your former employer should be increased in line with retail prices up to retirement.

* For members who join a scheme set up after the 1989 Budget or who joined any scheme from 1 June 1989, the maximum salary on which contributions and the benefits are based is £91,800 in 2000–1.

Source: based on Union Pension Services *Pension Scheme Profiles*

The good company pension scheme

Most people assume that if they join their company pension scheme it will provide a decent level of retirement income and other related benefits, but in practice final salary terms and benefits vary considerably. The same is true of money-purchase schemes, as discussed below.

If you want to check how your company pension scheme rates, consult your scheme booklet and compare the benefits listed with the ideal scheme in box 14.1.

Money-purchase schemes

There is a growing trend among employers in the UK to switch from final-salary pension schemes to money purchase, or to introduce a money-purchase option.

Money-purchase schemes allow employers to control their costs and also to transfer the investment risk to you, the scheme member. Now this is not necessarily a bad thing, but you do need to check the calibre of the administration and investment management companies running the pension scheme before joining. There are some excellent money-purchase schemes around, run by top firms of employee-benefit consultants and investment managers. But some insurance companies sell poor-quality schemes that combine dismal performance with high charges and inflexible contract conditions. Clearly, you need to know how to spot the difference.

One of the arguments employers use to justify the switch to money purchase is that employees do not understand final-salary schemes and therefore do not appreciate them. They are absolutely right and if you made your way through the first part of this chapter you can see why. However, one very important feature of final-salary schemes is that your employer is responsible for backing the pension guarantee and is obliged to contribute a variable amount to the pension fund to keep it solvent and able to meet its liabilities.

Money-purchase schemes can be attractive, especially for younger employees, because you have an identifiable pot of money which you should be able to take from job to job. Contributions are invested to build up a fund which, at retirement, is used to buy an annuity from an insurance company. An annuity pays an income for life in return for a lump sum.

The most important point to bear in mind with money purchase schemes is that, like personal pensions (see Chapter 15), the level of income your fund buys is not guaranteed but will depend on four factors:

- how much you and your employer contribute;

- the investment performance of the fund;

- the level of charges deducted from your fund by the pension company;

- annuity 'rates' – the level of income your fund will buy at the time you retire (annuity rates are based on the yields of long-dated gilts and bonds).

Companies that introduce money-purchase schemes do so in many different ways. Some employers close the old scheme and direct all future contributions to the new scheme. However, it is more common to introduce the money-purchase scheme for new employees and offer existing scheme members the choice. In some cases the money-purchase scheme will be open to younger employees who can join the final-salary scheme when they are older.

Bear in mind that pension transfers are notoriously complicated. If you are offered the chance to transfer your existing benefits from the old scheme to the new, do ask an independent pensions adviser or your trade union to check if it is a fair deal.

The good money-purchase scheme

Use the following checklist to find out if your employer's money-purchase scheme is well designed. It should:

- aim (but it cannot guarantee) to match the pension and risk benefits equivalent to a good final-salary scheme (see above);
- invest minimum employer and employee total contributions of between 10 and 15 per cent of annual salary, depending on age (you will need to pay more if you have not been contributing to a pension scheme all your working life);
- delegate the investment management to an institutional fund manager that has a proven track record in the pensions market;
- incur competitive administration and investment management charges;
- impose no financial penalties if you leave the scheme when you change jobs, you reduce contributions, or you want to retire early.

If you don't want to make the investment decisions, your scheme should also offer a 'lifestyle' option. This directs your contributions into equities in the early years to provide maximum potential for capital growth, but protects your fund as you approach retirement by automatically phasing a gradual switch from equities into cash and bonds.

Life cover under money purchase

Life cover under a money-purchase scheme should include a benefit linked to salary – for example three times annual salary. However, you may just be offered a return of your fund. If you have only been in the scheme a short while, this will not provide much of a pension for your spouse so it may be wise to increase your life assurance during the early years while the fund builds up.

Topping up

In most cases it is worthwhile joining your employer's scheme even if it offers skimpy benefits. This is because you will benefit from the company's contributions and, hopefully, the lower costs achieved through economies of scale. Remember, employers can contribute to your personal pension plan but they are under no obligation to do so. If you think you will not build up a decent pension you could top it up by increasing contributions to the main scheme or by paying additional voluntary contributions (AVCs – *see* page 169).

Group personal pensions

Group personal pensions (GPPs) are probably the simplest and most popular type of money-purchase scheme for employers. They also attract the largest rebates of NI contributions for those who want to contract out of Serps. GPPs are not classed as occupational schemes by the Revenue and in practice GPPs operate in the same way as individual plans, although a well-designed scheme should offer economies of scale.

Under a GPP, your individual personal pension plan can be used to contract out of Serps and to invest additional regular or single premiums to boost the pension provided by the NI rebate.

Personal pension contribution limits start at 17.5 per cent of 'net relevant earnings'

(equivalent in this context to pensionable pay) for employees up to age 35, and rising to 40 per cent for employees age 61 and over (*see* page 183). Employer contributions must be included in these limits, but there is no obligation for employers to pay anything.

The retirement income provided by the personal pension is not linked to final salary. Death-in-service benefits are not compulsory although the personal pension itself may provide a return of contributions plus interest. Extra life assurance can be taken out to increase this benefit.

The scheme provider

An increasing number of institutional managers are coming into the money-purchase market. These managers tend to delegate administration to a third party specialist. However, most money-purchase pensions are still run by insurance companies, which normally provide both administration and investment services combined.

Your employer should have taken expert independent advice and conducted a thorough analysis of different providers' financial strength, the management and commission charges, administration facilities, flexibility of contract terms and investment track record. If your employer accepted advice from a direct salesman or tied agent they would have received details about only one provider.

The charges

The scheme provider's charges will have a direct impact on the investment return and flexibility of your pension scheme. Where a standard life office package is used there may be large deductions in order to pay the high commission costs to the salesman or adviser, on top of which there will be administration and investment charges. Many advisers are prepared to rebate part or all of the commission in return for a fee and some will only work on a fee basis so that there is no deduction for commission. A good adviser will establish the most cost-effective contribution method.

Flexibility and portability

Flexibility is supposed to be one of the main attractions of money-purchase pensions since the employee has an easily identifiable and apparently portable pot of money. The important point to check here is what happens to your fund if you leave the scheme when you change jobs.

Long-term, regular premium life office contracts are notorious for their early termination penalties. Ideally your contract should have been established on a nil-commission basis or, alternatively, contributions should be paid on a 'recurring single premium' basis – that is a series of one-off investments – since the up-front charges are modest and there are no early termination charges.

Divorce

For most married couples the main breadwinner's company pension scheme benefits form the most valuable possession after the family home. Where the house is still mortgaged its net value often falls below that of the pension.

Over one-third of marriages in the UK end in divorce but until 1996 there was no legal obligation to split the main breadwinner's (usually the husband's) pension fairly. Instead, in England and Wales, pension rights were dealt with at the discretion of the courts. In contrast the law in Scotland is clear. Under the Family Law (Scotland) Act (1985) 'matrimonial property' specifically includes the proportion of pension and insurance rights accumulated during marriage and in most cases these must be divided equally between the partners.

The law in England and Wales is set to change. Since July 1996 the courts have been able to earmark the spouse's share of the pension and this will be paid out at retirement. Some time after 2000 (the precise date is not yet known), the court should be able to demand an immediate split of the funds so the lower earning spouse can invest his or her share of the pension into a personal pension fund.

This whole area is very complex and you should seek professional advice on the calculation of your pension rights, particularly if you or your spouse have built up a substantial pension.

Transfers

In the light of the personal pension mis-selling scandal (see page 180) you would be forgiven for thinking that employers with final-salary schemes are the good guys and insurance companies that sell personal plans are the bad and the ugly.

However, employers in the private sector who run the type of scheme that links the level of pension to salary are not exactly whiter than white when it comes to treatment of early leavers. Unless you fully understand the implications of your pension choices you could make an expensive and possibly irreversible mistake. Fee-based professional advice is essential, particularly where your pension transfer is high and your new pension arrangements are negotiable.

Pension choices when you change jobs

If you were in the pension scheme for less than two years you may be able to get a cash refund of your own contributions (less certain deductions), but not your employer's.

After two years you have the following options:

- you can leave the pension benefit in the former employer's scheme (known as a 'deferred' or 'preserved' pension) and draw the pension at retirement – there are many advantages associated with deferred pensions although much will depend on the generosity of the scheme both in terms of benefits that are guaranteed and benefits that are discretionary, that is, not guaranteed but paid on a fairly regular basis;

- you can take a transfer of benefits (the 'transfer value') to your new employer's scheme (*see* below);

- you can also take a transfer value to a personal pension, but remember you will lose out on the guaranteed link to salary and instead the value of your pension will be dictated by volatile investment returns – do not consider this route unless the two main options above are not appropriate.

If you are made redundant or are not sure how long you will stay in your next job, then you should leave the pension where it is until your future is more certain. Remember, transfers almost always cost money.

Summary

- It is almost always in your best interests to join your employer's pension scheme.

- If your employer does not run a scheme, check if there is an industry-wide scheme that you can join. Your employer or trade union should be able to point you in the right direction.

- Use the 'good pension scheme' guidelines in this chapter to see where your employer's scheme falls short.

- If necessary, top up your pension with additional voluntary contributions, free-standing AVCs or individual savings accounts.

- Make sure your family protection benefits are adequate and if not top up with private insurance arrangements.

Further information

The National Association of Pension Funds publishes a series of leaflets on company schemes and related issues. Many of these will be available free of charge from your pensions manager, but if not write to the association for a guide to its publications: NAPF, 12–18 Grosvenor Gardens, London SW1W 0DH (020 7730 0585; fax: 020 7730 2595).

The Trades Union Congress also publishes useful fact sheets on company pension. Write to the TUC, Congress House, Great Russell Street, London WC1B 3LS (020 7636 4030; fax: 020 7636 0632).

Transfers: an actuary is your best bet for help with transfers – try the Association of Consulting Actuaries (ACA) (020 7248 3163). Also consider a fee-based adviser who specializes in pensions. Try the Money Management Register of Fee-Based Advisers on 0870 0131 925.

chapter 15

Pensions – this time it's personal

Look, just because my hair is turning grey, and I'm getting flabby, my eyesight and hearing have diminished, my metabolic rate has slowed down, and I'm no longer producing braincells, doesn't mean I'm getting old.

Egon, *Extreme Ghostbusters* (1997)

After reading this chapter you will:

- discover that there is nothing magical about a personal pension – it is just a long-term investment with tax reliefs;

- realize that when it comes to pensions, governments work on the principle of trial and error;

- wonder why the government expects you to entrust your money to the very insurance companies that constantly screw up.

The politics of pensions is well demonstrated by the story of personal plans. In 1987 the Conservative government was so keen to wind down Serps (the second tier of state pension) that it give insurance companies free rein to sell personal pensions to anybody and everybody. Nor did the government check whether these companies were offering good value for money. Consequently, millions of plans were mis-sold and the industry is still mopping up the mess.

The Labour government then introduced Plan B. Its chief aim is to make available more group schemes organized on an industry, rather than single-employer basis. Industry-wide and stakeholder pension schemes are discussed on page 165.

However, this will still leave many people – particularly the self-employed – without access to a group scheme and the economies of scale they confer. For these people the government intends to encourage pension providers to offer simpler, cheaper and more flexible personal pensions than have been widely available in the past.

There is nothing new in these aims. Nor is there anything wrong with the concept of personal pensions. First-class providers have always offered a good choice of asset managers, flexibility and competitive charges.

This chapter explains how to get maximum flexibility and value for money. It also looks at performance – the one major aspect of personal pensions that the government cannot control. Without good performance all your hard work in selecting a pension plan will come to nothing. There is little comfort in knowing that you have had a flexible contract with low charges if, at retirement, the performance has been so poor your fund will not secure you a decent income.

So, before you buy a personal pension it is helpful to understand how these products work. For advice on how to pay for your plan and the impact this has on charges and flexibility, *see* Appendix 1.

How personal pensions work

Personal pensions do not provide a pension linked to final salary. Instead the plans operate on a 'money-purchase' or 'defined-contribution' basis which means that your contributions are invested to build up a fund that is used at retirement to buy an annuity. The level of guaranteed regular income you secure will depend on the fund size – and therefore performance – and how much the provider has deducted in charges, among other factors. It will also depend on annuity rates – that is, the rate of income per £1,000 insurance companies will guarantee. This is a wild card because annuity rates fluctuate and you have no way of knowing in advance what they will be when you retire.

To summarize, the main criteria on which your choice of personal pension should be based include:

- the performance track record, with the emphasis on consistently competitive annual returns over the long term;

- preferably access to a range of external investment managers;

- the flexibility of the contract – for example there should be no financial penalties for reducing and stopping contributions, transferring the fund and early retirement;

- the financial strength of the provider;

- the level of charges deducted during the lifetime of the policy;

- the cost of advice.

There are two component parts of a personal pension, although for the sake of convenience providers tend to lump these together. The 'appropriate' personal pension is used to contract out of Serps, while a 'top-up'

Remember the **good old days** when you could **just kill** your parents and **take** their land?

Carri, *Townies* (1996)

> **Mean money**
> There is little comfort in knowing that you have had a flexible contract with low charges if, at retirement, the performance has been so poor your fund will not secure you a decent income.

personal pension is used to take extra contributions in addition to the contracted-out rebate.

Like all pension arrangements approved by the Inland Revenue, the personal plan is a tax-efficient way of saving for retirement:

- contributions qualify for full tax relief;

- the pension fund grows virtually free of tax;

- up to 25 per cent of the main pension fund at retirement can be taken as tax-free cash – the rest of the fund must be used to purchase an annuity to provide the retirement income (the annuity can be bought at any age between 50 and 75).

Contracting out of Serps

If you want to opt out of Serps (see page 165) you need an appropriate personal pension.

Personal pension plans are designed primarily for two categories of employees:

- employees who do not have access to an occupational scheme;

- employees whose company scheme is 'contracted in' to Serps where the scheme benefits are paid in addition to the Serps pension.

The self-employed do not pay in to Serps and so cannot take out an appropriate personal pension.

These factors must be considered in conjunction with an important caveat: *if you earn less than £12,000 a year, under normal circumstances you should not opt out of Serps using an appropriate personal pension.* On these earnings your rebate is worth about £350–400 a year and you will find that most providers' charges will render this level of contribution uneconomic unless you also save through a standard personal pension (*see below*).

How the national insurance rebate is calculated

The NI rebate is calculated as a percentage of an employee's 'band earnings' – that is earnings between the lower and upper threshold for NI contributions (see page 71). For the 2000–1 tax year the NI thresholds are £76 per week (£3,952 per annum) and £535 per week (£27,820 per annum), giving annual

> **Mean money**
> If you earn less than £12,000 a year, under normal circumstances you should not opt out of Serps using a personal pension.

provider after the end of the tax year to which it relates. It is always worth checking that your provider receives this promptly since a delay in investment will reduce the returns. At the time of writing the DSS was experiencing severe delays in payments of NI rebates due to problems with the new National Insurance Recording System computer. However, it will automatically include compensation when it finally does make the payments.

'band earnings' of £23,868. The rebate ranges from just over 3 per cent to 9 per cent of band earnings, depending on age. So, the rebate for those earning £27,820 or over, would range from about £700 for young employees to about £2,150 at age 46 and over.

The rebate is sent by the Department of Social Security (DSS) direct to your personal pension

Standard personal pensions

In addition to the NI rebate, you can and should contribute a significant proportion of your earnings into a personal pension. The annual contribution limits are given in Table 15.1.

Table 15.1 Maximum annual contributions to a personal pension

Age	% earnings
Up to 35	17.5
36–45	20
46–50	25
51–55	30
56–60	35
61–74	40

Notes: The maximum annual contributions relate to the tax year and so will depend on your age on 6 April. All personal pension contributions are subject to the earnings cap, which limits the amount of salary that can be used for pension purposes to £91,800 for the 2000–1 tax year.

Old people **don't need** companionship.
They need to be **isolated** and
studied so it can **be determined**
what nutrients **they have** that might
be extracted for **your personal** use.

Homer, *The Simpsons* (1989)

It is possible to run more than one top-up personal pension plan provided total contributions fall within these limits. However, an employee can only have one appropriate plan for each tax year.

Your adviser should be able to help you assess the right contribution level but as a rough guide if you are under 30 you should be looking to pay in 5–10 per cent of your earnings.

Employer's contributions

Employers can contribute to an individual employee's plan, although there is no legal requirement for them to do so. Total contributions must stay within the maximum percentages shown in Table 15.1.

Life assurance

It is also possible to use up to 5 per cent of the contribution limit to pay for life assurance, which effectively gives you tax relief on the premiums. Life assurance rates vary considerably so do shop around. If your pension provider's terms are expensive, it might be cheaper to buy it elsewhere.

Insure against illness

It is important to protect your pension if you become too ill to work and can no longer pay the contributions. 'Waiver of contribution' insurance does just that and is vital. If you can no longer work, the pension company credits your fund with the contributions between the date your earnings stop and your retirement age.

Choice of personal pension plan

Personal pensions are available from dozens of financial institutions but the market is dominated by the life offices. An increasing number of unit trust and investment trust groups also offer their own personal pensions, as do some of the major institutional fund managers. Most banks and building societies tend to sell the plans run by their own life office.

A good-quality plan will offer you a default option that will automatically invest your money in assets suitable for your age. For example, young people generally are advised to invest 100 per cent in equities, but once you get within about ten years of retirement you need to start consolidating your gains and so gradually switch to gilts and bonds. For more details on investment choice, *see* Section 4.

Personal pensions with greater investment scope

One of the drawbacks with a standard personal pension is that in most cases you are restricted to the funds of just one institution. Given your pension plan could run for 35–40 years if you start young, this hardly seems prudent. All it takes is for your star fund management team to defect to a rival company and your returns could plummet.

Of course, if you are unhappy with the performance there is nothing to stop you transferring your plan to another pension company. Nothing, that is, except the exit penalties your pension company is likely to impose, particularly in the early years. On top of which you incur all the start-up costs with the new manager.

The government hopes to improve this situation by introducing what it believes is a new breed of funds based on unit and investment trusts, which do not incorporate all the upfront deductions of the traditional life office products. However, while the charges under unit and investment trusts are easier to understand and more flexible, they are not necessarily lower than life office funds.

Moreover, it is already possible to achieve greater investment flexibility and avoid the upfront charges. The following section looks at these existing opportunities, which hopefully will become more widely available as the government encourages – or even forces – providers to offer genuine flexibility.

Flexibility

The simplest way to keep the whip hand is to steer clear of any contract terms that tie you

Mean money
The level of guaranteed regular income you can buy at retirement will depend on the fund size – and therefore performance – and on how much the provider has deducted in charges, among other factors.

to your pension company. There are two ways to avoid high upfront costs and/or exit penalties:

- pay your adviser's charges by fees and ask for all commission payments to be stripped out of the contract;

- if you prefer the pension company to pay your adviser a sales commission, ask for 'single premium' terms – this means that each contribution is treated as a one-off and there are no large deductions in the early years to cover the adviser's charges over the full investment period (this is effectively what happens with unit and investment trusts).

If you follow these guidelines, in theory at least your plan should be very portable. When investment performance loses its shine you pick up your plan and take it elsewhere. However, there would by necessity be certain administration charges for starting up a new plan. so you need to take into consideration two further options when you choose your plan.

Access to external managers

A cost-effective method of achieving investment flexibility without having to transfer to a new company every time performance flags is to choose a pension plan that provides access to a range of external managers as well as the company's own funds. This approach was pioneered by

Skandia Life many years ago and today over a dozen life offices offer external fund links. In future this is likely to become a standard feature. In the market so far, apart from Skandia, are Merchant Investors Assurance, Professional Life, Scottish Amicable, Scottish Equitable, Scottish Life, and Winterthur Life.

However, do bear in mind that using a standard personal pension to gain access to institutional managers almost certainly will incur additional annual charges and therefore is more expensive than investing in a company's internal funds. Clearly, if this buys you superior performance and the flexibility to switch managers it is well worth the extra cost.

DIY plans

There is an option that offers even greater investment flexibility. If you are paying about £10,000 or more each year into your plan it is well worth considering a self-invested personal pension (Sipp) which allows you to separate completely the administration and investment management so that you can appoint your own investment manager (for example, a stockbroker) or even run the fund yourself. The beauty of this arrangement is that you can change your investment manager without disturbing the underlying administration and so cut out a significant layer of expense.

Sipps are also good news for professional practices and partnerships (Schedule D

Mean money

For the bigger investor a self-invested personal pension (Sipp) allows you to separate the administration and asset management. You can run the fund yourself or appoint an expert to do this for you.

taxpayers) who cannot join occupational schemes. It is possible to set up a group Sipp, which may enable you to negotiate lower charges and achieve a greater degree of investment control on a collective basis.

Sipps: the rules

Like personal pensions, Sipps are available to employees who are not in company schemes, to the self-employed and to partnerships.

With a Sipp you need to buy the basic plan from a specialist life office, which runs the administration. On top of this you appoint an investment manager to run the investment portfolio. In theory it is possible to handle the investment management yourself, but you should only undertake this task if you are an experienced investor and have the time to monitor stockmarkets on a regular basis.

Investment choice

The choice of investments is very wide and includes:

- stocks and shares (for example, equities, gilts, debentures) quoted on the UK Stock Exchange and including securities on the Alternative Investment Market;
- stocks and shares traded on a recognized overseas exchange;
- unit trusts and investment trusts;
- insurance company-managed funds and unit-linked funds;
- deposit accounts;
- commercial property.

A Sipp fund cannot purchase a firm's existing business premises from the partnership but it can buy new offices into which the partnership can move, provided the property is leased back on a commercial basis. You can also use your Sipp fund to borrow on the strength of its assets to help with property purchase. However, the Sipp cannot lend part of the pension fund back to you, the investor.

Fee-based advice

The merits of fee-based advice, particularly where higher contributions are involved, are discussed in Appendix 1. A professional adviser, remunerated by fees, should be able to arrange nil-commission terms where life office funds are used.

Also, the higher premiums associated with Sipps, particularly where they are arranged on a group basis, should make the fee approach cheaper in the long run. This is because conventional pension contracts that combine investment and administration normally make an initial charge based on a percentage of your contributions.

Summary

Standard plans

Don't:

- Consider opting out of Serps with an 'appropriate' personal pension if you earn less than £12,000 a year.

- Rely on the investment of the national insurance rebate to provide you with a good pension. You will need to top up with extra contributions.

- Buy a personal pension if you have access to a good company pension scheme. Company pensions generally represent better value for money and usually provide good death and disability benefits as well.

Do:

- Seek help from an independent financial adviser (*see* Appendix 1).

- Check the past performance results thoroughly (ask to see the independent surveys and not the provider's interpretations of these results).

- Seek advice on the choice of fund. Younger people should invest more in equities but older people should usually gradually switch to safer investments such as gilts.

- Check the flexibility of the plan. You should be able to reduce or stop contributions or transfer to another provider without penalty.

- Pay a sensible amount into your personal pension plan if this will be your main source of retirement income.

- Try to get your employer to contribute. This is something to ask your new employer if you are about to change jobs.

- Boost your life assurance through your personal pension if appropriate, since you will get tax relief on the premiums. Shop around first though – in some cases the personal pension provider might charge high rates for term assurance and it may be cheaper to get it elsewhere even without the tax relief.

Flexible plans

- Look for a pension plan that offers a choice of external investment managers.

- For the bigger investor a self-invested personal pension (Sipp) allows you to separate the administration and asset management. You can run the fund yourself or appoint an expert to do this for you.

- Partnerships can set up a Sipp on a group basis and even use the fund to purchase new business premises.

chapter 16

Your money and your life

Some people will pay a lot of money for that information, but then your daughter would lose a father, instead of gaining a husband.

Michael Corleone,
The Godfather (1972)

After reading this chapter you will:

- be very glad your employer provides all this expensive stuff;

- understand why small print gets such bad press;

- feel like you have a price tag on your head – and be right.

Mean money

The amount of life assurance you buy must be geared to your liabilities. As a rough guide you could multiply your salary by 10 to provide a lump sum for your dependants which, when invested, will generate a reasonable replacement annual income.

This is a very grown-up and sensible chapter – which is why it's at the end. It's not about you but your family, so we are assuming a minimum level of responsibility here. For the simple fact is that if you have any dependants who would suffer financially as a result of your death or disability then you really do need life assurance and income protection.

If you are lucky, your employer will provide all of this stuff as part of your benefits package. But if you are self-employed or work for a small company that does not offer a standard employee benefits package, you need to buy private insurance policies.

Life assurance

The 'sum assured' – the amount of cover you take out – should do two things:

- repay any outstanding loans including the mortgage;
- allow your family to maintain its standard of living by replacing your income in full or by topping up any other benefits you may receive.

How much do you need?

The amount of cover you buy must be geared to your liabilities. As a rough guide you could multiply your salary by 10 to provide a lump sum for your dependants which, when invested, will generate a reasonable replacement annual income. A more precise method is to calculate the income you actually need to meet expenditure, including the cost of outstanding loans.

Consider carefully the period you need to insure. One way of looking at this is to cover the period during which any borrowing remains outstanding and until the children have ceased to be dependent – up to the age of 23 if you expect them to go to university. Don't forget that where there are young children, the partner responsible for childcare must also be insured. The cost of a full-time nanny could easily run to £8,000 a year.

The basic calculation then is 'income requirement plus debt minus any existing cover'. Existing cover may be provided by your company pension scheme or other private insurances. Company pension schemes can provide up to four times the level of your annual salary as a tax-free cash lump sum if you die. They should also provide a spouse's pension and possibly a pension for your children if they are under 18.

Personal pension plans also provide life cover. However, in this case the value will not be linked to your salary but instead will depend on how much is in your fund. If you have only recently started a pension plan this could be very little, so you will need to pay for extra life assurance while your fund is building up. You can also use up to 5 per cent of your personal pension contribution allowance to pay for life assurance.

The main drawback with life assurance linked to your company pension scheme is that it only applies while you are working and contributing. If you are in this position, make the most of it while it lasts, but be prepared to top up with private insurance if your employment circumstances change.

In particular, make sure the cover provided by your old and new jobs overlaps. A common mistake is to go off for a holiday between jobs and to forget to arrange stop-gap insurance.

Which type of policy?

Once you identify the shortfall in your provision you can use one of the methods listed below to fill the gap.

The two simplest products are level-term assurance and family income benefit. The term

You want me to seduce a dying girl? And what makes you think she'll just leave me all her money?

Merton, *Wings of the Dove* (1997)

assurance lump sum can be invested to provide an annual income and/or used to pay off debt, while family income benefit can directly replace the shortfall in annual income.

Most life assurance policies work on the 'you drop dead, we pay up' principle. However, some companies offer whole-of-life plans, which combine insurance and investment by deducting the cost of life cover from your savings plan.

The following descriptions explain your basic options.

Level-term assurance

Level-term assurance provides a tax-free cash lump sum if you die within the period insured. However, if you die the day after the term expires you get nothing. Unless the policy is assigned to cover a specific liability – for example your mortgage debt – it is sensible to write it under trust so that the lump sum does not form part of your estate if you die. In this way the policy proceeds could be passed on to your children, for example, without having to wait for probate to be granted to your executors.

Life assurance can be written on a single or joint-life basis. A joint-life policy covers more than one person – typically a husband and wife. It may be written to pay out if just one of the spouses dies ('joint life first death') or only when both have died ('joint life second death'). Experts reckon it is usually better – and only slightly more expensive – to arrange individual policies.

Remember, wherever you share ownership you have an insurable interest and it is important to take appropriate cover. Young people often buy houses together to share the cost, while older couples may purchase a holiday home with friends.

Term assurance also comes in other forms:

- *Convertible renewable term assurance* gives you the right to extend the insurance period without further medical underwriting or, in some cases, to convert to an investment linked plan. The former can be useful if you need to increase your life cover when you are older. Generally you would be asked to undergo a medical and could pay much higher premiums if you are not in good health.

- *Decreasing term assurance* reduces at regular intervals and can be used to protect a debt that reduces in a similar way – for example, where the outstanding debt decreases over the loan period at regular intervals. However, repayment mortgage protection insurance is structured in a slightly different way to accommodate the specific pattern of the capital debt reduction (*see* page 199).

- *Increasing term assurance* automatically increases the level of cover, usually in line with retail price inflation or a fixed amount – say, 5 per cent – without further medical underwriting. If you opt for this type of insurance your annual premiums will also increase.

- *Personal pension term assurance* is available to the self-employed and employees not in company schemes. Premiums attract full tax relief provided they fall within your overall annual contribution limits. However, if you stop earning, you must also stop the plan. As mentioned above, although you can use up to 5 per cent of your annual pension contribution allowance to pay for life assurance, you may not want to do so if you need to pay the maximum amount to your pension plan.

Family income benefit

Family income benefit (FIB) provides a regular income from the date of death until the end of the insurance period. Tax treatment is favourable because although the proceeds are paid in the form of a regular monthly income, technically they are classed as capital so there is no income tax to pay. You can arrange for the income to remain the same ('level'), or to increase each year. FIB is particularly useful where you have a young family and you want to insure the life of the spouse who stays at home to look after the children, so if he or she dies you can afford to employ a nanny and/or continue the school fees payments.

Whole-of-life plans

As the name suggests, whole-of-life plans pay a benefit whenever you die: there is no specific term. Given the certainty that the policy must pay out at some point, naturally the premiums tend to be higher than for term assurance. Whole-of-life policies combine insurance and investment. Your monthly premiums are invested and from this fund the insurance company deducts the amounts necessary to provide the life cover. When you die you get the fund value or the sum assured, whichever is greater. One common use for this type of policy is to provide a lump sum to cover your inheritance tax liability when you die.

Tips on buying your life assurance

As a general rule it is better to avoid products that combine insurance and investment. If what you need is a sensible amount of life cover then simple term assurance is likely to offer best value. If you want to build up some capital for your dependants you could, for example, invest in tax-efficient individual savings accounts (Isas) and take out a decreasing term assurance plan to provide a lump sum if you die early before your fund has had a chance to build up.

The premium you pay for your insurance will depend on your age, sex and your state of health, among other factors. You have a duty to complete the proposal form honestly and accurately. If you are considerably overweight or you smoke, your premiums may be 'loaded' – in other words you pay more because there is a greater chance of an early death. Certain dangerous sports will also raise eyebrows in the underwriting department and in turn may raise your premiums. In some cases your policy may not cover you while you indulge in these activities.

The proposal form will also ask if you have ever been tested for HIV (AIDS). If you are a single man and want a substantial amount of cover you will probably be requested to complete a 'lifestyle' questionnaire that is designed to discover whether your private life exposes you to a higher than average risk of AIDS or other sexual diseases.

The medical

Both men and women who want to take out a large amount of cover should expect to be asked to undergo a medical examination. Despite the aversion most people have to this,

it does actually work in your favour. Where policies are not fully medically underwritten (this is usually the case with policies sold by direct mail or through off-the-page advertising) the underwriters assume there will be a much greater incidence of claims so the premiums may be much higher than a medically underwritten contract.

The premium will also depend on the company. Life assurance is a very competitive market, which is why independent advice is essential. These days good advisers will have access to a comprehensive database that will enable them to select the right features and the best rates available at any given time.

Your adviser should also make sure your premium rate is guaranteed. The cheapest rates often are offered by companies that reserve the right to 'review' premiums at any time. With reviewable premiums, effectively you are writing the insurance company a blank cheque.

How to pay

You may be offered a choice of payment options – for example you could pay annually by cheque or monthly by direct debit. Direct debit is probably the safest method because the payments are guaranteed. If by mistake you overlook a reminder for your annual cheque your cover may lapse and if you have to re-apply you may find that rates have increased due to your increased age or a change in your state of health.

Mean money

Most life assurance policies work on the 'you drop dead, we pay up' principle. However, some companies offer whole-of-life plans, which combine insurance and investment by deducting the cost of life cover from your savings plan.

Income protection insurance

Life assurance protects your family if you die but it is equally important to insure against loss of income due to illness or disability. If you are not convinced, consider this. In April 1995 the government cut long-term sickness benefits and changed the definition of qualifying disability from 'can't do *own* job' to 'can't do *any* job'. This means that even though your medical condition prevents you from continuing as a brain surgeon, if you can sweep the streets you will be classed as fit for work.

The change in the eligibility rules wiped an estimated 250,000 people off the list of the 1.6 million who previously claimed the old invalidity benefit. The new incapacity benefit is taxed and if your claim started after 13 April 1995 you will not get an earnings-related top-up, previously worth up to £85 per week.

This leaves not so much a gap in welfare provision as a gaping chasm. If you are not covered by a group scheme, you need private insurance.

There are two products that protect you if you become seriously ill or disabled. 'Income protection plans' (also known as 'permanent health insurance' or PHI) provide a regular income, while 'critical illness' insurance pays out a lump sum on diagnosis of a serious condition. A third product you will come across is mortgage protection insurance, which essentially is a combination of the two.

Price is the crucial factor when you buy insurance, but independent advice is essential given the range of products and the complex medical underwriting criteria applied by the insurance companies.

Income protection plans

Income protection or PHI pays a maximum of about two-thirds of your earnings (less any state and company benefits) if you are prevented from working through disability or long-term illness. The income is tax free and is payable for the full period insured, which is usually up to the date you start to draw your pensions.

This type of insurance should itself carry a health warning, as the policies often are live on while you are waiting for your income protection plan to kick in.

Advisers stress it is essential to link the insured income to retail price inflation – both during the insurance period and during the payment period. This will cost extra but without it the purchasing power of your income would quickly be eroded.

Misleading contract features

With PHI there are two vitally important but potentially misleading contract features – the premium basis and the definition of disability.

The premium basis

An apparently cheaper policy may have a 'reviewable' premium. As mentioned in the previous chapter, this means that you have no control over future rate increases. Over 40 companies sell PHI but only a handful, including Sun Alliance, Friends Provident and Swiss Life, at the time of writing offered premiums guaranteed not to rise.

Several companies sell investment-linked PHI policies, which review premiums in line with claims experience and investment returns. They may also pay a lump sum at the end of the insurance period. However, these complex products are not necessarily cheaper than the guaranteed premium version. As a general rule it is wise to keep your investments separate from your protection insurance.

riddled with small print. The premium you pay will depend on age, sex, occupation and level of earnings covered. Most insurers will only cover earnings of up to about £45,000, so high earners may not be able to fully protect their income.

If you are on tight budget, to keep premiums down you could insure the minimum income you need to survive and increase cover later (but first check your policy will allow you to do this). You can also cut premiums if you opt for a long waiting period between the date you fall ill or become disabled and the date you claim benefit. The minimum waiting period is four weeks but premiums reduce if you sign up for a three, six or 12-month 'deferment' period. If you opt for a long deferment period then make sure you have enough savings to

The definition of disability

This is the deciding factor when the insurance company judges whether you are too ill to work and therefore are eligible to claim benefit. The best definition is 'unable to follow *own* occupation' with the possible addition of the phrase 'or an occupation suitable by training, education, experience and status'. The worst definition (to avoid at all costs) is 'unable to follow *any* occupation'. Under the latter you have got to be totally incapacitated in order to claim – as is now the case with the state scheme.

Critical illness insurance

Critical illness insurance is often regarded as the poor man's PHI. This type of insurance pays the owner of the policy – which could be you, your spouse or even your business partner – a tax-free lump sum on the diagnosis of up to 36 illnesses or accidents. Most policies use six standard definitions:

- cancer
- heart attack
- stroke
- coronary artery bypass surgery
- kidney failure
- major organ transplant.

> I'm 4064 years old. What do you think I owe it to – a terrific moisturiser?
>
> Saul, *Soap* (1977)

If you are self-employed, the best way to protect your family, should you become too ill to work, is through a PHI policy. Critical illness may be a cheaper way to insure against some of the worst possible illnesses but unless your condition is on the list you will not receive a penny, even though you are unable to work. A good critical illness insurance policy will include 'permanent total disability' on the payment list.

Mortgage payment protection

There is nothing unique about mortgage protection plans – these are usually a combination of term assurance and a restricted version of PHI or critical illness insurance.

Term assurance is the simplest way to provide mortgage protection as this pays off the loan if you die. A special type of decreasing term assurance can be used where the debt reduces with time – as is the case with a repayment mortgage. For an interest-only loan, where the debt remains constant throughout the mortgage, you need level-term assurance.

Where the policy you are offered includes an element of income protection, do check your existing cover first. If you take out more term assurance than you really need, at least your family will reap the benefits. However, if you over-insure with some of the income protection plans, you are not entitled to the excess, so some of your premiums will be wasted. As a rule, advisers reckon it is usually better to buy term assurance and critical illness or PHI separately to provide the right type and level of cover.

Another option you may be offered is accident, sickness and unemployment (ASU) insurance. This covers your monthly mortgage payments if you become too ill to work or are unemployed. The accident and sickness element is like a short-term PHI policy. Unemployment insurance is available through a few specialist companies but is very expensive, so ASU may be the only way to get it.

Following social security changes, if you are a new borrower and become unemployed you now have to wait nine months before you can claim benefit to cover your mortgage – longer if you have savings of £8,000 or more. You can use ASU to insure the nine-month gap and in some cases can cover yourself for up to two years. However, experts warn that you should treat this type of insurance as a way of buying some breathing space if you need to reassess your finances in the light of illness or unemployment. It does not provide a long-term replacement income.

Mean money

The best definition of disability is 'unable to follow *own* occupation'. Avoid policies that say they will only pay up when you are unable to follow *any* occupation. Under the latter you have got to be totally incapacitated in order to claim – as is now the case with the state scheme.

Summary

Life assurance

- If you have dependants who would suffer financially if you die, you need life assurance.

- As a rough guide to how much cover to take out, multiply your salary by 10, add in the value of any outstanding loans and deduct any existing cover, for example from a company pension scheme.

- Don't forget to top up your life assurance if your company benefits package changes when you change jobs.

- Take out life assurance for the spouse who looks after the children. If he/she dies you will need to pay for childcare or work part time.

- Opt for a guaranteed premium. Some companies retain the right to 'review' (upwards) the premium whenever they want to.

Income protection

- You can only claim state incapacity benefit if you are unable to do *any* job.

- Income protection or permanent health insurance plans can be used to replace up to two-thirds of your regular income.

- Specialist advice is essential – these policies are riddled with small print and vaguely worded clauses about pre-existing conditions.

- Make sure the premium rate is guaranteed not to rise or is restricted to the rise in inflation. 'Reviewable' premiums can be increased at any time.

- The definition of eligibility for benefit should be 'unable to continue *own* job'.

- A good critical illness policy will include 'permanent total disability' on the eligible conditions list.

Help!

You're walking around blind without a cane pal. A fool and his money are lucky enough to get together in the first place.

Gekko, *Wall Street* (1987)

How to choose your financial adviser

The UK is not short of advisers. In fact you could say it is rather over-blessed with the breed. Unfortunately, the financial services regulators do not publish a list of 'jolly good' ones so it's down to legwork. This Appendix describes the different categories of advisers and Appendix 2 gives the addresses of organizations worth contacting to get you started in your search.

Which type of adviser?

This is very important. It is virtually impossible to judge character but you *can* judge what sort of advice a company or individual is authorized to offer because you can simply ask and they have to tell you. If you can get the hang of this you will be doing a lot better than most of the population, which still thinks bank managers are nice guys and give independent advice. They're not and they don't.

Company representatives

Company reps (also known as direct salesmen and tied agents), as the name implies, are employed by – and work solely for – just one company. Their income usually comprises two elements – a basic salary and a commission element.

Some representatives are remunerated purely by sales commission, which means if they don't sell you a policy they don't eat. In recent years financial institutions have been under pressure to move away from this system and most now pay reasonable basic salaries so there is less need to verbally beat you into submission. Where commission is paid, the amount will depend on how much you agree to invest in a product and for how long.

Buying direct is not a bad thing. Some of the best pension products – as well as some of the worst – are sold in this way. Several notable newcomers to the pensions scene – including Virgin, Marks & Spencer and Tesco – sell direct and claim to offer good value for money as a result.

The important point to remember is that direct sales advisers by law are only permitted to sell the products of the company they represent and through which they are authorized. So, if you are after a personal pension, you will not be told about the other 99 products available with their 99 different charging structures and 999 different fund links.

In conclusion, buying direct is worth considering if you are confident you know what to look for and can research the market thoroughly. But if you buy blind on the grounds that you like the record label, the underwear or the croissants, frankly you are taking a gamble.

Appointed representatives

These are the companies that have a contract with a life office or other financial institution to sell one or more of its products in return for commission. The appointed representative is not necessarily employed or owned by the life office and may act independently in other lines of business.

A typical example of an appointed representative is a building society that offers an independent mortgage service but only sells the endowment and personal pension products of one life company (often its own). So, if you want an endowment mortgage you will borrow XYZ Building Society's money but there will be no choice of endowment products – you will have to take the ABC Life Assurance endowment, or lump it.

The appointed representative will tell you that the company is authorized to sell the endowment/pension products of just one company. Like the company representative, he/she is not obliged to tell you how competitive that product is in terms of charges and performance.

Independent financial advisers

Independent financial advisers (IFAs) are not tied to one life assurance company. Their job is to examine your needs and to search the market for the product that offers the best value in terms of performance, charges, and contract flexibility, among other factors.

For this reason, in theory at least, you stand a better chance of coming away with the right

The cheaper the crook, the gaudier the patter, eh?

Sam Spade, *The Maltese Falcon* (1941)

financial products than if you go to a company or appointed representative. However, the term 'independent' is not synonymous with 'expert'. IFAs vary considerably in their level of competence.

Your choice of adviser will be dictated partly by your pocket and partly by your preferred investment route. If you are interested in a self-invested personal pension and want to invest directly in equities as well as collective funds (unit trusts, investment trusts and insurance funds) then you will probably require the services of a stockbroker or investment manager. If you plan to invest purely in collective funds, what you need is a well-resourced and experienced firm of independent financial advisers.

Use the contacts in Appendix 2 to draw up your shortlist of firms. Obviously, the cost of the advice is important and you should ask for a rough estimate before proceeding.

Paying for advice

Advisers vary in the way they are remunerated. Some IFAs are remunerated entirely by commission paid by providers on the sale of products. Others – including the professional firms – are remunerated entirely by fees paid directly by clients. Yet others take part of the commission and a reduced fee for each sale. And then there are those who will operate on a commission or a fee basis depending on your preference: if you want to pay a fee, that's fine, but if you want to pay by commission that's fine too. Helpful, perhaps. Confusing, certainly.

Fee-based advisers charge anything from around £50–250 per hour depending on whether you go to a local high-street adviser or a leading firm of consulting actuaries. As a rough guide however, for good pensions advice you can expect to pay at least £80–130 per hour, with an overall minimum total of about £300–500 depending on the nature of the case and the seniority of the adviser. As mentioned, commission rates vary depending on the size of premium and the term of the contract, so the more you plan to invest the more likely it is to be cost effective to pay a fee.

It's easy to get bogged down in the commission *v* fees debate and frankly not worth the time. The purists argue that if you want to make sure that your adviser is not influenced by the levels of commission available on different products, then the best route is the fee-based adviser. The pragmatists argue that for many people, the level of fees charged by professionals is a deterrent.

Whether you pay fees or commission, the important point is to know what the total bill is likely to be and whether the commission structure makes your plan inflexible if you want to reduce or stop payments.

The client agreement

If you plan to use your adviser on a regular basis it is a good idea to have a written agreement that sets out the firm's terms and what services it will provide. A clearly worded client agreement gives you a benchmark against which you can judge the adviser's performance, particularly where the firm has direct responsibility for investing your money. For example, is the adviser monitoring the performance of your individual or small company pension plan and if so what action has he or she taken to offset any problems on charges and performance? Are you receiving regular updates on performance?

The following checklist includes the main points in a client agreement. You should add any further points that apply to your particular circumstances.

- The regulation of the adviser under the Financial Services Act 1986.

- The services the adviser is entitled to carry out and the services they are not authorized to undertake. For example, is the adviser authorized to hold client money or custodial investments?

- Permission – required by the Consumer Credit Act (1974) – for the adviser to act on your behalf to negotiate mortgages, loans and overdrafts.

- The period of agreement and period of notice on both sides (usually a minimum of 30 days).

- Your responsibility to provide the information the adviser needs (for example, the adviser needs a list of your existing investments and you need to be clear about your attitude to investment risk).

- The adviser's access to your other professional advisers, for example your bank manager, accountant and pension provider.

- Your right to veto any recommendations.

- A confidentiality clause.

- Details of how your documents will be stored.

- Fee rates per hour for different level of advisers within the firm and details of any due dates for regular fees.

- Details of VAT likely to be charged.

- Treatment of commissions if the adviser acts on a fee basis. Does the firm reinvest this money or offset it against fees?

- Treatment of complaints and disputes.

Summary

- The main factors that affect your annual return are performance and the cost of your investment, including the advice.

- Unless you are sure of your ability to research the market thoroughly, seek independent advice.

- Consider which type of firm is suitable – for example do you need a stockbroker to advise on direct equity investment or would you be happy with one of the firms of advisers that specialize in collective investments such as unit and investment trust plans?

- Check the level of qualifications held by the staff and the firm's research resources.

- Ideally pay for your advice by fees rather than commission, as this removes any potential bias in the firm's recommendations.

Financial planning
and
investment advisers

Advice is cheap
Ms Malloy. It's the things
that come gift
wrapped that count.

Horace, *Hello Dolly!* (1969)

Where a telephone number is not provided the organizations below prefer you to contact them by post. Before you appoint a firm to act on your behalf, you can check with the chief regulator, the Financial Services Authority (FSA), that it is authorized and registered with the appropriate regulator. To contact the **FSA central register**, telephone 020 7929 3652. www.fsa.gov.uk

Stockbrokers and investment managers

The Association of Private Client Investment Managers and Stockbrokers publishes a free directory of member firms, many of which provide a full financial planning service. Contact APCIMS, 112 Middlesex Street, London E1 7HY. The APCIMS directory is available on www.apcims.co.uk. E-mail info@apcims.co.uk

Financial planners and advisers

The Institute of Financial Planning is multidisciplinary and its members are well qualified in giving independent planning advice. Contact the IFP at Whitefriars Centre, Lewins Mead, Bristol BS1 2NT. For the register of fellows of the institute, telephone 0117 930 4434.

The Society of Financial Advisers is part of the Chartered Insurance Institute and is a major examiner of independent advisers and life assurance company sales staff. Use the 'Find an Adviser' service on www.sofa.org or contact SOFA at 20 Aldermanbury, London EC2V 7HY (020 7417 4419).

Independent advisers: for a list of three local independent advisers, contact **IFA Promotion** on 0117 971 1177 or www.ifap.org.uk. For fee-based independent advisers contact the **Money Management Register** on 0870 013 1925.

Accountants

About 700 members of the Institute of Chartered Accountants are qualified to offer a full advisory service but members of other taxation bodies can also help.

The Institute of Chartered Accountants in England & Wales, Moorgate Place, London EC2P 2BJ (020 7920 8100/8711). www.icaew.co.uk

The Institute of Chartered Accountants in Scotland, 27 Queen Street, Edinburgh EH2 1LA (0131 225 5673).

The Association of Chartered Certified Accountants (ACCA), 29 Lincoln's Inn Fields, London WC2A 3EE (020 7242 6855). www.acca.org.uk

The Chartered Institute of Taxation and Association of Tax Technicians, 12 Upper Belgrave Street, London SW1X 8BB (020 7235 9381). Chartered tax advisers and members of this institute specialize purely in tax work for companies and for individuals (020 7235 9381). www.tax.org.uk

Solicitors

The Law Society of England & Wales, 113 Chancery Lane, London WC2A 1PL (020 7242 1222). www.lawsociety.org.uk

The Law Society of Scotland, 26 Drumsheugh Gardens, Edinburgh EH3 7YR (0131 226 7411).

The Law Society of Northern Ireland, Law Society House, 98 Victoria Street, Belfast BT1 3JZ (028 9023 1614).

Solicitors are strongly represented in the financial services market. Two organizations dedicated to professional independent advice are:

Solicitors for Independent Financial Advice (SIFA), telephone the helpline 01372 721172. www.solicitor-ifa.co.uk

The Association of Solicitor Investment Managers (ASIM), Chiddingstone Causeway, Tonbridge, Kent TN11 8JX (01892 870065).

Pension specialists

The Association of Consulting Actuaries, Number 1 Wardrobe Place, London EC4V 5AH (020 7248 3163). www.aca.org.uk

The Association of Pension Lawyers (APL), c/o Eversheds, Senator House, 65 Queen Victoria Street, London EC4V 4JA (020 7919 4500).

Other useful organizations

The Association of Investment Trust Companies (AITC) is the trade body for investment trusts. Its directory, *The Investment Trust Handbook*, is available from PBI Publishing (020 7638 1916). There is also a *Unit Trust and Oeic Handbook*. AITC, Durrant House, 8–13 Chiswell Street, London EC1Y 4YY (020 7431 5222).

The Association of Unit Trusts and Investment Companies (AUTIF) is the trade body for unit trusts and open-ended investment companies. It publishes a range of free fact sheets that explain how these investments work. AUTIF, 65 Kingsway, London WC2B 6TD (020 7831 0898). www.investmentfunds.org.uk

The Stock Exchange publishes useful leaflets on buying and selling shares and on rolling settlement and nominee accounts. The Stock Exchange, London EC2N 1HP (020 7797 1000). www.londonstockexchange.com

Complaints

Under the Financial Services Act, if a company sold you an inappropriate product for your needs you may be able to claim compensation. Not everything is regulated business. For example, protection products are classed as general insurance so if you have a complaint contact the Insurance Ombudsman (020 7928 7600). The banks and building societies also have their own ombudsmen (0345 660902 and 020 7931 0044).

If you have an investment complaint, write to the compliance officer at the company which sold you the product. You should receive an acknowledgement of your letter within seven days but allow two months for the actual investigation before taking the case to the ombudsman or regulator.

The company's letter head should show the details of the regulator but if not, contact the Financial Services Authority central register (*see* above) or write to:

The Financial Services Authority, Gavrelle House, 2–4 Bunhill Row, London EC1Y 8RA. Consumer helpline: 0845 606 1234. www.fsa.gov.uk

Where
there's a
will there's
a relative

I am Susan Ivanova ... I am the right hand of vengeance and the boot that is going to kick your sorry ass all the way back to Earth, goddammit! I am death incarnate and the last living thing that you are ever going to see. God sent me.

Ivanova, *Babylon 5* (1984)

213

For most people, making a will is a simple and cheap exercise, and represents a small price to pay for your own peace of mind and for the ease and comfort of your family. Yet only one in three adults bothers.

If you meet your maker without a valid will you die 'intestate' and the laws of intestacy will decide which of your dependants receive your money, while your friends and favourite charities will receive nothing. In particular, if you have young children you will not have had chance to make careful arrangements for their inheritance of capital (this would instead happen automatically at age 18 under the intestacy rules), and you will not have appointed the executors, the trustees and the children's guardians who will oversee their upbringing.

Remember also that there are certain events that render it essential to rewrite your will – in particular if you get married or divorced. As a general guide, even if there are no major changes relating to marriage or children, it is worth checking your will is up to date every five years.

Making a will does not involve a huge amount of work, unless your finances are very complicated. Most solicitors do the legwork for you and simply ask you to complete a short form that provides the information they need to draw up a draft.

What happens if you don't make a will

The main disadvantages of dying intestate are:

- your estate may not be distributed in accordance with your wishes;
- the appointed administrators may not be people whom you personally would have chosen – or even liked;
- it may take longer for the estate to be distributed, whereas when a will has been made the executors can take up their duties immediately after death occurs;
- the costs may be greater, leaving less to pass on to your beneficiaries;
- children will receive capital automatically at age 18, whereas you may have preferred this to take place later at a less 'giddy' age;
- the family home where your widow or widower lives may have to be sold in order to raise the capital;
- a testamentary guardian is not appointed for young children;
- trusts may arise under an intestacy that produce complications, including statutory restrictions on the trustees' power to invest and advance capital.

Points to consider

When making a will, there are several common mistakes that can be easily avoided. For example, you should make sure you dispose of all your estate because if you do not then this could result in partial intestacy. You should also make provision for the fact that one of your main beneficiaries may die before you. Above all else, consider the legal rights of your dependants. If you do not make suitable provision then they may be able to claim their right to a sensible provision under the law. Remember in this context that 'children' refers to legitimate, illegitimate and adopted children, although it does not usually include stepchildren. You should also include any gifts to charities or specific gifts of assets to specific beneficiaries (for example your jewellery to your daughter/granddaughter).

Don't forget you can use your will to make some important arrangements about your own wishes. For example, if you have a strong preference for burial or cremation, and know where you wish to be buried/your ashes to be scattered, this is the place to make your wishes known.

The trust powers of the trustees should also be set out. You should discuss any specific role with an appointed executor or trustee before you put it in writing. These responsibilities can be onerous or may conflict with some other role the individual already performs. Where you have young children the appointment of willing and responsible guardians is essential, particularly where only one parent is alive.

Finally, if you own any property overseas you should draw up a will under the terms of that country, with care to ensure consistency with your UK will.

Executors and trustees

The executor is responsible for collecting your estate and distributing it in accordance with the law. This can include paying any outstanding taxes and dealing with other financial affairs. The executor takes over from the date of your death but is not officially appointed until the will is 'proved' and the appointment is confirmed by a grant of probate.

Most people appoint as an executor a spouse or close relative plus a professional – for example your solicitor or accountant. Where the will includes a trust it is helpful if the executor and the trustees are the same people.

Distribution of an estate under the laws of intestacy

The following details refer to the law in England and Wales. The laws that apply in Northern Ireland and in Scotland differ. 'Issue' refers to children (including illegitimate and adopted), grandchildren and so on. It does not include stepchildren.

If the deceased dies leaving:

- *A spouse but no issue, parent, brother, sister, nephew or niece*: the spouse takes everything.

- *A spouse and issue*: the spouse takes £125,000, personal 'chattels' (car, furniture, pictures, clothing, jewellery etc.) plus a life interest – that is the income only – in half of the residue. The children take half the residue on reaching age 18 or marrying before that age. In addition, on the death of the deceased's spouse, the children take the half residue in which the spouse had a lifetime interest.

- *A spouse, no issue, but parent(s), brother(s), sister(s), nephew(s) or niece(s)*: The spouse takes £200,000, plus personal chattels, plus half the residue. The other half goes to whoever is living in order of preference: parents, but if none, brothers and sisters (nephews and nieces step into their parents' shoes if the parents are dead).

- *No spouse*: Everything goes to, in order (depending on who is still alive): issue, but if none, parents, but if none, brothers and sisters (nephews and nieces step into their parents' shoes). The pecking order then moves on to half-brothers and sisters or failing them, their children, but if none, grandparents, but if none, uncles and aunts (cousins step into their parents' shoes), but if none, half uncles and aunts (failing that, their children). If all of these relatives have died then the estate goes to the Crown.

Where part of the residuary estate includes a dwelling-house in which the surviving spouse lived at the date of death, the spouse has the right to have the house as part of the absolute interest or towards the capital value of the life interest, where relevant.

Further information

This chapter is based on Section 14 of *Kelly's Financial Planning for the Individual* by Simon Philip, published by Gee Publishing Ltd. Sections reproduced are by kind permission of the author.

Summary

- Only one in three adults has made a will in the UK.
- If you fail to make a will you will cause delays in the distribution of your estate and you have no control over the choice of beneficiaries.
- Do use expert help when you draw up your will. A DIY will, unless very carefully worded, may prove invalid, in which case the laws of intestacy apply.
- Make sure all the important details about your professional advisers and your financial affairs is set out for your executors.